WEAVING WOMEN

WEAVING WOMAN

Essays in Feminine Psychology
from the
Notebooks of a Jungian Analyst

Barbara Black Koltuv, Ph.D.

NICOLAS-HAYS
York Beach, Maine

First published in 1990 by
Nicolas-Hays, Inc.
Box 612
York Beach, Maine 03910

Distributed to the trade by
Samuel Weiser, Inc.
Box 612
York Beach, Maine 03910

Library of Congress Cataloging-in-Publication Data

Koltuv, Barbara Black.
    Weaving woman / Barbara Black Koltuv.
      1. Women—Psychology. 2. Jung, C.G. (Carl Gustav),
  1875–1961. 3. Psychoanalysis. 4. Femininity
  (Psychology) I. Title.
  HQ1206.K594 1990
  155.6'33--dc20   90-6736
                                       CIP

ISBN 0-89254-019-2

Cover art is part of a private collection and is used by
permission of the artist.

Typeset in 11 point Bembo by
Sans Serif, Inc.
Printed in the United States of America by
Baker Johnson, Inc.

For Hannah

Table of Contents

Preface

These essays have been a long time in coming: weaving begins, perhaps, in wool gathering, in conception, or in stringing the loom. Material must be gathered, a structure provided, and a process of washing, carding, sorting, designing, weaving, tightening, sometimes undoing and reweaving carried out.

Five of these essays were conceived in 1973 as a seminar series for the C.G. Jung Foundation in New York. It was called "Weaving Woman." I wanted to give the seminars for women only, but the director of the foundation at that time, a woman, was uncomfortable with this concept. She agreed not to publicize the series as for women only, but to accept only women. As might have been predicted, the only people who wanted to take the course were women. Two years later, I added three more lectures and the Foundation offered "Weaving Woman" again. By then, times had changed, I had changed, and there was no need of a women-only seminar space. One man registered for the course, but he only attended the first week.

During the past seventeen years, the material in these lectures has been sorted, carded, discarded, added to and redesigned, but the process and the essence have remained the same. *Weaving* is the process, and *woman* is the essence.

I have been an analyst for a quarter of a century, and a woman for twice that many years. Learning, understanding, and finding meaning have been central in my life and have been accomplished, both alone with myself, and in relationship with others. My patients are mostly women, and my friends, too, are mostly women. They have shared their deepest experiences and self-knowledge with me as I have with them. There are also the others, who are men. With them the experiences are often more intense, full of feeling and passion, but the sharing is less frequent and perhaps more precious because it is so rare. One learns differently in encounter with the opposite, Other.

—Barbara Black Koltuv
1990

Chapter One

BLOOD MYSTERIES

Imagine a being that bleeds but is not wounded. Imagine a being that bleeds but does not die. Is it a magical, mythical creature, or merely a woman? Or both? Can such a being be "merely" woman? There is a certain mystery here, of which man can know nothing, and women must know something:

> How can a man know what a woman's life is? A woman's life is quite different from a man's. God has ordered it so. A man is the same from the time of his circumcision to the time of his withering. He is the same before he has sought out a woman for the first time, and afterwards. But the day when a woman enjoys her first love cuts her in two. She becomes another woman on that day. The man is the same after his first love as he was before. The woman is from the day of her first love

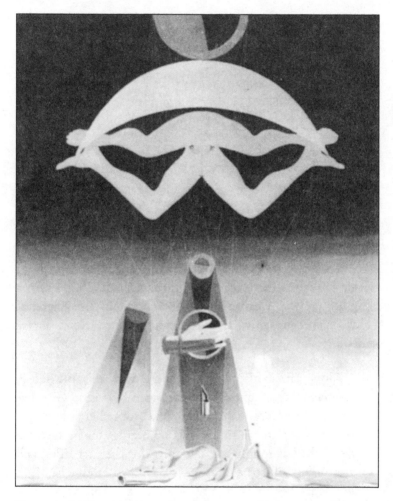

Figure 1. *Of This Men Shall Know Nothing*, Max Ernst, 1923, oil on canvas. Tate Gallery, London.

another. That continues so all through life. The man spends a night by a woman and goes away. His life and body are always the same. The woman conceives. As a mother, she is a person other than the woman without child. She carries the fruit of the night for nine months in her body. Something grows. Something grows into her life that never again departs from it. She is a mother. She is and remains a mother even though her child dies, even though all her children die. For at one time she carried the child under her heart. And it does not go out of her heart ever again. Not even when it is dead. All this the man does not know; he knows nothing. He does not know the difference before love and after love, before motherhood and after motherhood. He can know nothing. Only a woman can know and speak of that. That is why we won't be told what to do by our husbands. A woman can only do one thing. She can respect herself. She can keep herself decent. She must always be as her nature is. She must always be maiden and always be mother. Before every love she is a maiden, after every love she is a mother. In this you can see whether she is a good woman or not.[1]

I begin with these words from a noble Abyssinian woman because her expression is so authentic that the usual arguments about nature and nurture, biology and destiny, become irrelevant. At a basic biological level women *are* different: we have a moon cycle. We are capable of carrying and nurturing another life within ourselves, and of giving birth and nourishment from our own bodies. This is the miraculous transformative aspect of women. This inner moon cycle, or menstrual cycle, affects our energy, our ideations, our emo-

Figure 2. O Lady Moon, your horns point toward the east:
Shine, be increased.
O Lady Moon, your horns point toward the west:
Wane, be at rest.

Christina Rossetti, "Lady Moon," 1892

Illustration from *Women: A Pictorial Archive from Nineteenth-Century Sources* (New York: Dover Publications).

tions, and is the matrix of our very nature. This lunar cycle affects all women, to some extent, and men, too, through their contrasexual side. It affects some women more than others. For women, it is an ever present essential inner gyroscope. A fact of life. When you reach up, or in, and grab hold of the horn of the moon you have access to the deepest level of Self. (See figure 2.)

This moon nature is a certain quality of time and experience that consists of change, process, and transformation that is rhythmic and periodic, cyclical rather than linear. Lunar time waxes and wanes. Things seem propitious, or not. They are right at one time and wrong at another. Matters are relative and interrelated. Much of one's life is this way, that is, governed by lunar time more than by the more abstract, quantitative precision of always, never, or certainly of rational solar time. A woman wrote this about lunar consciousness:

> I learned that I knew this truth when my second baby was a few weeks old and my husband and longtime companion (who was also a clinical psychologist, but of a more rational quantitative disposition) asked, "When will he sleep through the night?" In the fifteen years since we had attended graduate school where the scientist-practitioner model reigned supreme, I had become a mother and I *knew* for sure how thunderously unaskable his question was.[2]

By knowing this, and taking hold of one's inner moon cycle, one can remain true to oneself, *and* to one's relationships to others. One can experience the lunar depths rather than the silvery, fickle, sickle surface. Moreover, by attending to one's inner cycle, women are less likely to be burned alive while mistakenly emulating mad dogs and Englishmen who go out in the noonday sun. The popular expression "burn-out" seems an accurate term for the results of the cultural overvaluing of the solar, and neglect of the lunar, myth. The Qur'an knows each to be God's signs, of equal value, or favoring night. When prayer is offered in the last third of the night, darkest night, Layla-Allah comes down to the lowest God Heaven — closest to mankind — so He can be sure to hear the prayers of humans.

A Kabbalistic creation myth explains that in the beginning the Sun and Moon had equal light and power, but they fell into a jealous lover's quarrel. God, in order to settle their dispute, diminished the Moon's light and made her go forth as "one that veileth herself." There were eons of consequences[3] to this seeming diminishment and veiling of the moon's power

Figure 3. The warring lovers, Sun and Moon, with Moon already veiled. From *Aurora Consurgens*, a 14th century alchemical text.

and light, and of course, the lover's quarrel of the Sun and Moon continues still. (See figure 3.)

The moon and our own inner moon cycle is intimately related to creativity. In order to gain access to the level in ourselves we must first acknowledge that it *is* a mystery, a Blood Mystery that must be approached with a religious attitude. The moon's quality of mystery of being veiled and hidden is also, I believe, an essential aspect of woman's nature. For example, a woman in the throes of a magnificent love affair dreamt[4] that she and her lover had been parted by their parents, their fates, and society—as in Romeo and Juliet. An older woman—actually her lover's mother, who had raised her children and then returned to her native land (Norway, the land of the midnight sun) to live out her own life—puts her in touch with her lover for a few moments, but then the connection is broken. Although the older woman, a switchboard operator in the dream, begins to try to reestablish contact, the dreamer leaves in search of kohl eyeliner to rim her eyes, or veil her soul. There was a need for this *separatio* of the lovers so that the woman could connect to herself. The dreamer had first begun to wear kohl in Fez, a labyrinthian city in Morocco. Anaïs Nin wrote in her second diary that Fez is the image of the city of the interior—the image of her inner self: "the city which looked most deeply like the womb with its Arabian Nights gentleness, tranquility and mystery. Myself, woman, womb, with grilled windows, veiled eyes. Tortuous streets, secret cells, labyrinths and more labyrinths."[5] See figure 4 on page 8.

The dream had told the woman that her inner "mother-in-law," operating in solar time at the rational technological level was trying to connect her to the outer man, while she herself, on lunar time, needed to wander the inner labyrinth of

Figure 4. Veiled women from various cultures.

her feminine nature in search of kohl, a leaden substance used since ancient times to rim the eyes, or windows to the soul.[6]

In the Bible women prepare for heroic acts by applying kohl in a ritual of ceremoniously costuming and masking one's inner intent: *not* as a way of making oneself attractive to others, nor as a way of "fixing" oneself or of becoming acceptable. In Old Testament times, when people were closer to their earlier matriarchal goddess-worshipping cultures, women still made cakes to the Queen of Heaven, the moon (Jeremiah 7:18). Women got in touch with their feminine creative power by veiling themselves.

Esther prepares for a terrifying encounter with the king, a course she has chosen against his divine patriarchal rule by withdrawing, meditating, and applying kohl and other magical potions (see figure 5 on page 10). Thus, she saves her people, our Judeo-Christian ancestors, from annihilation. Yael retreats into her tent, applies kohl and other unguents, and then invites Sistera, the enemy of her people, in. She feeds him milk and honey and makes him sleepy. Then she drives a tent peg through his skull. Judith, too, applies kohl and veils herself. Then she seduces and decapitates the enemy of her people and carries his head home in a basket. Tamar also ritualistically paints her eyes, veils herself, disguising herself as a prostitute, and waits by the side of the road to force her father-in-law to do what she believes is right and just.

Later historically, Jezebel's painted veiled eyes and her feminine power are decried. And in the New Testament, Salome *un*veils herself in a ritual dance to obtain John the Baptist's head on a platter. Is this perversion of the deep instinctual feminine need to veil oneself an expression of collective feminine wrath at the coming of a Christian age, where the son of God carrying all the Solar light values is born of a

Figure 5. *La Toilette d'Esther*, Theodore Chasseriau, 1842. The Louvre, Paris.

virgin standing on the crescent moon and women are denigrated as sinful temptresses, or idealized as vessels for *kinder*, *kuch*, and *kusch*? Women suffering from solar burnout dream of tiled communal changing rooms at high school gymnasiums and "health" clubs, resembling those of ancient Greece, that are frequently invaded by "the guys" and offer no privacy or facility for veiling or unveiling. As these modern women come more in touch with their feminine lunar nature, the changing rooms of their dreams become more protected and harem-like (see figure 6 on page 12).

The moon is an analogy to woman. It is different each night and has a regular, though mysterious, cycle. Our view of the moon changes. Sometimes it is not there at all, unseen, hidden and veiled, yet it rules the tides of emotion and energy. By becoming conscious of the inner moon or menstrual cycle we can partake of the goddess within and begin to know ourselves. By consciously *submitting* to the inner necessity of our instinctual life, we become most individual, most true to ourselves. This is what Esther Harding called the psychological attitude of Virgin—one in herself[8]—or what Irene de Castillejo calls our feminine soul, that which cannot be denied.[9]

The beginning of the cycle is like a crescent moon waxing,[10] building up estrogen. There are feelings of initiating, building, energy, strong sexual desire, a turning outward ascendent mood. At midcycle, ovulation, the time of the full moon, erotic feeling is at its fullest, deepened with a powerful receptivity, tense with desire. It is a time for loving, open, easy orgasms. Women feel good, confident and strong. At this time, a woman dreamt of a silver-haired dog running toward her, coming over the top of a lovely rounded hill. Estrogen levels are high and progesterone levels are rapidly

Figure 6. Full moon altar. Photo courtesy of Haskin-Lobell.

increasing; psychologically there is an intensification of the receptive retentive tendencies that represent a preparation for pregnancy. It is a good time to work on projects begun earlier. A good time for relationships.

Then suddenly, one Sabbath later, estrogen and progesterone levels decline sharply, the dark of the moon is upon us! Women experience tension, anger, strong urgent sexual needs (at the same time that we are driving our lovers away with our shrieking). Androgens are in the ascendancy. Depression, despair, fears of mutilation and rage abound. All the primal forces are upon us — and within us. It is a time to withdraw, retreat and introvert. A time to go inside oneself. Imagine a menstrual hut at the edge of a swamp. During a premenstrual week, a woman dreamt: "There is a small house in a clearing in the woods. Crude, redneck men stand around the clearing awaiting the running of the bulls. The dreamer, feeling the wild violence and bloodiness of the impending action, goes into the house."

This introversion, a going inside of one's Self and withdrawing from a masculine or patriarchal value system, can be a time of great self-healing, creativity, and spirituality. A time of women's mysteries. A woman can retreat and work on what is needed for the next turn of the wheel. The need for this feminine introversion and connectedness to the goddess is reflected in the story of Rachel in the Old Testament. She stole the household gods from her father's house. These were earthen images of the Great Goddess Astarte. When her father came to where she and Jacob were camped and wanted to search for the stolen idols, Rachel hid them under her camel litter, and sat on them. When her father came into the tent to search for the Goddess, she said "Do not look angry, my lord, because I cannot rise in your presence, for I am as women are from time to time and every now and then." Rachel remained seated, as it were, on her own feminine nature, while her father searched the camp, but could not find the idols. Patriarchal law, the rule of Yahweh, prohibits men from coming near, touching or accepting food from a menstruating woman. Even sitting on the couch of a menstrual woman was forbidden because one might sit where she had sat. Perhaps these taboos reflect the fear of the neglected, rejected Great Goddess' magical Blood Mysteries and power.[11]

This being seated upon one's own feminine nature, and the concurrent introverted process required during the premenstrual days, is an interior psychological shift. If one consciously accedes to the process, there are great benefits; if one doesn't, the Goddess' wrathful rage is felt in painful consequence. A woman consciously related to her inner lunar cycle continues to work, relate to others, and live her life, but she relates from a different, darker, deeper place. This is not a disease syndrome. This is a naturally occurring, biologically determined, culturally beneficial, necessary cyclical event. Women, and their men, who consciously accept this periodic need to withdraw and shift levels, reap tremendous rewards. They find premenstrual week energy is great for cleaning up piles of easy, usually boring, repetitive physical tasks. It's a time for gathering, sorting, cleaning, easy, methodical stuff. It is not good for fine discrimination, reasoning or quick decisions. It is the time to clean out closets, drawers, and refrigerators.

Relating to the Blood Mysteries of one's own instinctual feminine nature connects women to themselves, the human condition, and the Goddess within. Charlotte Painter, in her novel *Who Made the Lamb*[12] tells the story of an American woman anthropologist who became pregnant while living in a

14

small village in Mexico. Although the woman had lived there for more than a year, she had no part in the life of the village. When her maid conveyed the news to the women of the town, they approached the anthropologist, and using a beer bottle to represent the baby, taught her how to wrap, hoist, carry and nurse a baby in a *rebozo* or shawl. She felt suddenly that she was a woman among all the women of the world. These blood mysteries—menstruation, sexuality, pregnancy, childbirth, lactation, and menopause—are our history within ourselves and in the world.

When one begins to consciously take hold of the moon, and to sleep with one's face turned moonward, she rewards us with her light and fecundity. This very personal and detailed dream journal and case history is the only one included in the book. It demonstrates how practical and informative attention to the inner moon cycle can be. The dreamer is a 36-year-old woman, mother of a year-old baby boy and a 7-year-old girl. She was a psychotherapist in training to become a Jungian analyst, and a patient of mine.

The experience began with a dream of being connected by a wire from a mysterious source to a wart on my left index finger. It didn't hurt but it made me aware of the wart and curious about the connection—where it led, what it meant . . .

A few days later, I dreamt of making a descent down a steep mountain path, carrying my young son in my arms. It was raining heavily and I was very afraid of losing my footing. Sylvia appeared and told me that she had been there before and that there was another way to go. She showed me that by turning to the left the path was not so steep. "But I want to go down," I told her. She assured me that it was still a descent, and I followed her way.

Sylvia is the name of the eldest of the Vestal Virgins and the Sylvia in the dream is the woman who first told the dreamer the story of the descent of Ishtar. In the myth, Ishtar, as Queen of Heaven and Earth, longing for her son/lover Tammuz, descends to the depths and darkness of the underworld, which is ruled by her twin sister, Irkalla. There are seven gates to be passed through on this journey and at each place Ishtar must remove one of her garments or jewels.

Padraic Colum's telling of the story conveys the rhythm and poetry that are so much a part of the experience of lunar time:

> "Enter, O Lady, and let the realm of Irkalla be glad at thy coming; let the palace of the land whence none return rejoice at thee." He said this and took the great crown off Ishtar's head. "Why hast thou taken the great crown off my head?" "Enter so, O Lady; this is the law of Irkalla."

The ritual continues at each of the gates until . . .

> . . . the Lady Ishtar, her head bent, the radiance gone from her, no longer magnificent in the gold of her ornaments, with apparel no longer full nor resplendent, with stumbling and halting steps went through the sixth gate and saw the seventh wall before her. The Watchman opened the gate that was there. "Enter, O Lady. Let the realm of Irkalla be glad at thee; let the palace of the land whence none return rejoice before thee." He said this, and he took off her garment. "Why hast thou taken off my garment?" "Enter so, O Lady; this is the law of Irkalla."

16

And naked, with her splendour, and her power, and
her beauty all gone from her, the Lady of the Gods came
before Irkalla. And Irkalla, the Goddess of the World
Below, had the head of a lioness and the body of a
woman; in her hands she grasped a serpent.[13]

There followed dreams of being pulled voluptuously down-
ward. She dreamed of traveling through "locks" of a canal to
descend still further, guided by a Hecate-like woman who told
the dreamer of biting her 4-year-old daughter when the child
was in the midst of an Oedipal temper tantrum one mid-
summer day in a very conservative Maine coast resort town.
In another dream she heard of a woman who went down to
"Lower Westchester" to pick up her son, and died there.

Then there were dreams about all sorts of dreadful
shadow qualities—a Terrible Mother figure, negative, critical,
deprived, and deadly, and her consort the gross, earthly, phallic aspects of the masculine expressed in the statue of Bacchus
illustrated in figure 7 on page 18.

In her waking life, too, she encountered the dark and the
negative. She found herself forced to deal with another mother
in her son's playgroup whom she intuitively tried to avoid.
There was uncanny coincidence of personal history between
that mother and the Terrible Mother of which she dreamt.
Both their mothers had died in childbirth, both were aban-
doned by their fathers in Europe twice—in early childhood,
and again later at 13 or 14. Both had not wanted children and
had hysterectomies and many other serious operations while
still relatively young women.

During this period, my patient felt that she was truly in
the underworld. She felt that her nose was being rubbed in the
earthy, the gross, and the negative. While Ishtar, during her

Figure 7. The gross and earthly Bacchus. This statue is at the Pitti Palace, Florence.

stay in the underworld "saw the light no more; feathers came upon her; she ate dust and fed upon the mud; she was as one of those she had sent down into Irkalla's realm."[14]

And then to her despair, my patient realized that she was pregnant. She was only a day or two late, but she knew. It was such a fitting punishment, she felt, because she considered the conception of each of her children as a miracle and because her experiences of pregnancy and childbirth had been the most numinous of her life. Here she was pregnant, she said, knowing she would have to get an abortion. She would have to consciously decide to use the negative power of the Goddess to abort this baby because she knew she could not give it the love and care it would need.

She dreamed of being in the underworld and meeting an earthy woman named Pearl Pluto, who had been a friend of hers around the time of puberty. Pearl's older brothers and father were butchers. The name Pearl, too, was over-determined: during this period the dreamer was working on a needlepoint design of a dragon descending from heaven into the sea to bring forth a flaming pearl, that she associated with the Gnostic myth of the pearl of individuality which is rescued from the depths. She thought of Sylvia Plath's "Ode to Lesbos" in which she speaks of Jewish mothers who guard their sons' sweet sex like a pearl.[15]

In the next dream, dressed in silken garments, she encountered the Other, a cold and impersonal man whom she loved and respected, who says, as he's about to make love to her, "I hope you haven't fouled the sacred precinct." He seemed to be saying, "You must not get an abortion because it is against God's will," a heavy patriarchal judgment. She fought against the weight of it.

That weekend she planned to attend a seminar by Joseph Campbell about the Great Goddess. She dreamt that she came to the seminar, and there were all the Jungian analysts in New York. One of them, a young woman, was prancing about with freedom and joy as she had recently done while presenting a paper about her experience of embodiment through movement. In the dream she was the leader of the workshop and told those in attendance to choose a partner. The dreamer asked whether she would be her partner and suddenly, magical symbols appeared, representing wholeness of the masculine and feminine elements as in the Yin and Yang.

That evening, my patient attended the actual seminar, and Joseph Campbell, showing a slide of ancient bull dances, said that worship of the Goddess is always characterized by living experience, dance or sacrifice, rather than by heavenly dogma.

In life, too, she began to experience the positive, nurturing, related aspects of the feminine, and of other women. The Vestal Virgin woman, Sylvia, who had originally guided her in her descent dream, suggested that she find a ritual for saying goodbye to the baby—from her own experience of regret at not having done so when she had had an abortion. A feeling, very motherly friend told her that if she found herself pregnant, she also would have an abortion because she knew that having a baby now would overwhelm her. That night she dreamt that the motherly woman had to help perform the abortion by turning a Pre-Colombian green jade stone on a pivot. The stone was inscribed with ancient Mayan symbols. The Great Round turned, and the decision was made.

The day she had the abortion, two new patients called. Both of these people needed to deal with death. One was a woman who had been given her name by another therapist two months earlier. The woman had had an abortion, and then a year later a still-born child. The other was a former patient who had worked with her five years earlier when he first contracted Hodgkins disease. She hadn't been able to do much then, but he returned now, she felt, as a sign that perhaps she could now help him face living with death.

The final dream was this: an image of herself as a clay figure, seen from a distance, dressed in black and white, wherein she found the meaning of her experience of the Goddess. The dreamer, with the help of the Goddess within, was able to make the decision to have the abortion. Ten lunar months later she dreamt of dead babies, trays and trays of bodies of dead babies, and had to come to terms with the patriarchal Judeo-Christian God who lives within us also — but that is another story.

Chapter Two

MOTHERS AND DAUGHTERS

"Blood Mysteries" is about the underlying essential wholeness of the feminine psyche. The next two essays, "Mothers and Daughters," and "Hetairae, Amazons and Mediums," approach the psychology of women a little more analytically using Toni Wolff's "Structural Forms of the Feminine"[1] as an informative classification scheme. Each woman has, I believe, each of these qualities within her. She develops, differentiates and lives out of each of these energies or roles at different times of her life. With biology as our guide, we will begin at the beginning, with mother and daughter. There are strong emotional ties here. One never quite separates from one's mother. After years and years of analysis and self-understanding, one is liable to come upon a strand of feeling that ties one irrevocably to one's mother. One hears her voice come out of us in speaking to a child or

Figure 8. Eve, mother of all, in a decidely Persephone mood. *Eve,* Lucien Levy-Dhurmer, 1896, pastel and gouache.

one glimpses her face in the mirror in a certain expression, or feels oneself to be a helpless, enraged child at the age of 30 or 40 or 50. Older women especially say, "I'm becoming my mother." Jung writes,

> Demeter and Kore, mother and daughter, extend the feminine consciousness both upwards and downwards. They add an "older and younger," "stronger and weaker" dimension to it and widen out the narrowly limited conscious mind bound in space and time, giving it intimations of a greater and more comprehensive personality which has a share in the eternal course of things. . . . We could therefore, say that every mother contains her daughter in herself and every daughter her mother and that every woman extends backwards into her mother and forwards into her daughter. This participation and intermingling give rise to that peculiar uncertainty as regards *time*: a woman lives, earlier as a daughter, later as a mother. . . . An experience of this kind gives the individual a place and a meaning in the life of the generations, so that all unnecessary obstacles are cleared out of the way of the life stream that is to flow through her. At the same time the individual is rescued from her isolation and restored to wholeness.[2]

Novels, films, dreams, and experience illustrate this essential continuity (see figure 8). Here is a dream of a woman who had what is called a negative mother complex. She had determined to be anything but like her mother. Therefore she had problems separating from her mother, and also in differentiating and respecting her own needs and desires. I think it is more often true than not that women with "anything but like mother complexes" marry their mothers, or at least often marry men who are very like their mothers in the way they relate to them. In the case of this dreamer this was certainly true.

She had the following dream on the night when she was finally able to say "no" to sex with her husband because she was not in the mood. She dreamt that her mother appeared wearing the same type of eye makeup (kohl) around her eyes that the daughter used. The daughter admired the mother in the dream and saw her beauty, as well as her own resemblance to her mother. The mother says she has to take her sister-in-law Sarah, her husband's sister, to the hospital because she has cancer. The dreamer's associations to Sarah included references to Sarah in the Old Testament (whom she felt was often victimized by Yahweh's power plays as he manifested himself to her husband Abraham). Like many females in the Book of Genesis, Sarah had great difficulty conceiving, perhaps because there was such intense suppression of the matriarchal Goddess-centered religions. She was an essentially motherless female of the early patriarchy.

When God's three angels visited Abraham and told him that Sarah would conceive, she laughed. She was 93, but she did conceive eventually, and bore Isaac, whose name means "she laughed." When God told Abraham to sacrifice Isaac, he would have done so without question and without regard for Sarah's feelings in the matter. He did not even tell her when he took Isaac to Mount Moriah to kill him. Also, possessively, Sarah drove the handmaid Hagar and her son Ishmael away, even though Sarah had asked Hagar to conceive and bear Abraham's child when she did not believe she herself would conceive. The dreamer's personal associations to her Aunt Sarah were also interesting in that she thought Aunt Sarah was a very selfish, bitter, possessive, masochistic mother type who not surprisingly was being eaten alive by cancer, the devouring feminine life force turned against itself.

Because the daughter, the dreamer, had been able to say "no" to her husband out of respect for her own needs and desires, the mother within her had been transformed and was now beautiful herself. The inner mother was now willing and able to help *her* husband's sister (the Sarah shadow side) get the healing treatment she needed. Yes, it's endless, like the concentric circles in a pool of water created by the intervention of a single pebble.

The same ambivalent deep interconnection and need for differentiation is expressed by Adrienne Rich in her marvelous book *Of Woman Born*:

> I saw my own mother's menstrual blood before I saw my own. Hers was the first female body I ever looked at, to know what women were, what I was to be. I remember taking baths with her in the hot summers of early childhood, playing with her in the cool water. As a young child I thought how beautiful she was; a print of Botticelli's Venus on the wall, half-smiling, hair flowing, associated itself in my mind with her. In early adolescence I still glanced slyly at my mother's body, vaguely imagining: I too shall have breasts, full hips, hair between my thighs—whatever that meant to me then, and with all the ambivalence of such a thought. And there were other thoughts: I too shall marry, have children—but *not like her*. I shall find a way of doing it all differently.[3]

Rich adds:

> Probably there is nothing in human nature more resonant with charges than the flow of energy between two bio-

logically alike bodies one of which has lain in amniotic bliss inside the other, one of which has labored to give birth to the other. The materials are here for the deepest mutuality and the most painful estrangement.[4]

To me the myth of Demeter and Persephone best illustrates the mother/daughter archetype within us and the psychological issues of separation and individuation it raises. Briefly, here is the myth, told most fully and beautifully in the Homeric Hymn to Demeter:

Persephone, the much loved daughter of Demeter the Goddess of fertility, is with her friends gathering flowers. The earth Goddess Gaia, in order to please the Lord of the Underworld Hades, causes a narcissus to spring up. A hundred blossoms spread from its root, a sweet fragrance spreads around it and Persephone is seduced away from her friends. When she reaches for the flower, the earth opens, a chasm appears, and the Lord of the Underworld carries her off to his dark realm.

Persephone's screams are heard by Demeter, but she does not know what has transpired. She grieves and searches for Persephone and finally goes with Hecate to Helios, the Sun, who tells her that Hades has abducted her daughter with Zeus's consent. Demeter, grief stricken, leaves Olympus to dwell amongst men. Clad as an old woman, she sits beside a well in Eleusis where she is engaged as a nurse for a boychild. The baby grows miraculously. His mother becomes suspicious and spies on Demeter one night as she holds the child in the flames to burn off his mortality. The mother cries out to her son in terror, "I must mourn and lament you." Demeter, enraged, finally reveals herself as a Goddess, reproaches the

28

woman for her ignorance of this fact and demands that a temple be built in her honor at Eleusis.

The temple was built and Demeter sat in it mourning for her lost daughter. In her sorrow and rage she caused no food to grow on earth. She would destroy all mankind with evil famine unless Zeus forced Hades to return Persephone.

Hermes is sent to retrieve her, and although Persephone had previously refused all food while in the realm of the dead, after she hears of her liberation and reunion with her mother, Persephone eats three pomegranate seeds, thus ensuring her return to the underworld and her lover Hades for at least one quarter of the year.

In the joyous and loving reunion of mother and daughter, the earth is covered with a new and blessed greenness, and Demeter in her beneficence vows to teach her mysteries to mankind.

What drew me to this myth originally was the violent image of the earth splitting and Persephone's abduction. This forced descent to the underworld, the violent initiation into sexuality, the feeling of being dragged kicking and screaming into the depths, is a frequent experience of women in adolescence, in love, and in analysis. This feeling, and the symbolic elements of the Demeter/Persephone abduction rape myth appear so often in women's dreams that they seem to be an essential, natural and organic part of women's separation and individuation process.

Demeter is to me *the mother*, epitomizing the maternal quality in women that has been extolled in our unique ability to nurture and support all that is young and growing in others. Philip Zabriskie, in his paper, "Goddesses in Our Midst,"[5] points out that it is this kind of mothering that fosters the self-acceptance that makes a child say, "I'm glad to be me." The same mothering quality has been deplored in endless novels and psychological theories because of its anxious, over-protective, masochistic, guilt-inducing, power motivated, crippling effects. Neumann describes it as the elementary character of the feminine. "It is the Great Round or the Great Container. It tends to hold fast to everything that springs from it and to surround it like an eternal substance. Everything born of it belongs to it and remains subject to it; and even if the individual becomes independent the Archetypal Feminine *relativizes* this independence into a nonessential variant of her own perpetual being."[6]

Demeter contains within her Persephone, a cherished young, innocent, virginal, protected aspect of herself that reaches for a new sensuous experience — the flower. One feels that her innocence needs to be effaced. Gaia, the older form of the earth mother, remember, grows the flower *for* Hades. It is as though nature on a deeper, more ancient level accepts the need for the violent upheaval of change.

The abduction and rape robs Demeter (or the motherly quality in ourselves) of its innocent maidenly quality. Where we are *too much mother* in relation to a man, children, friends, lovers — to anyone, even things or projects — we can feel the banality, the conventionality, the too much sweetness and light, the niceness. This generality needs to be crossed by the vertical, downward-pulling experience of abduction and rape by Hades, an experience of the underworld that brings with it a connection to the "transformative aspect of the feminine."

But that gets to the happy ending a bit too fast. First we have Demeter's reaction to the need for change — a heavy, depressed anger turned against herself. She withdraws. A patient of mine, a mother type — whose lover did not meet her expectations and who needs to celebrate her birthday —

30

depressed, too tired to do anything for herself, fantasized buying perfume for me, not for herself, and next year being away from home and friends for her birthday so she wouldn't be disappointed. This is typical Demeter behavior. She becomes a nursemaid for another woman's baby. When she is thwarted in her sublimation—her attempt to make *him* Godlike and immortal—she blows up. And finally "becomes" herself—a Goddess. She demands obeisance, acknowledges who she is and says what she wants. This is the real turning point in the myth and, psychologically, the time when we sacrifice the easy love and approval we get for being good women or girls, and recognize and express our own needs and wishes.

Another patient was married to a narcissistic man, much like her mother, who could not love her. She finally told her husband that she could no longer live with him. During their long marriage she had grown in loving self-acceptance and found that she could care for her own needs quite easily and happily. Very soon she found a profoundly loving, giving and accepting love relationship with another man. She dreamt:

> I go uptown to the street where I had been together with my new lover to meet my husband. As I get out of the cab I realize that I haven't brought my overnight things. [She hadn't stayed overnight with her lover because she feared being too quickly overwhelmed by her feelings for him.] It's 6:00 o'clock. Rush hour. I must hurry to my husband. I can return for my things later, I think. I find my husband in a three room suite. He is in a cold white-tiled, sterile bathroom. He sits huddled in the corner on the closed toilet lid, naked, knees up in the fetal burial positions of corpses I had heard of left for a year in caves around Jerusalem during the first and second century. I

31

have arrived at just the right moment. I sense that he is neither dead nor alive. I reach out and touch my palm to his face. He is neither warm nor cold. I take both his hands in mine and pull him into life for the last time. Then, I must leave him. I traverse the center space and enter the far room. There, wrapped in a pink and gold numinous glow, is a young girl of 14. A virgin, in a silken quilt or cocoon. I must be with her, now.

This dream marked the end to her loveless, mother-complected marriage of death, and the beginning of her new life, true to herself.

When Demeter was able to use her goddess-given, fiery anger and nourishing power to demand that Persephone be restored to her, the masochistic knot was broken. This knot consists of doing for others, not being appreciated, feeling angry, depressed, full of self-pity, unloved but not loving oneself enough to do what one wants. Demeter says, "no," finally, "no, nothing for anyone," until she gets her daughter back!

The last part of the psychological story that I just love is that Persephone *chooses* then to eat the pomegranate seeds, thereby acknowledging that she *is* different now. The Demeter/Persephone quality is more differentiated and has been transformed by Persephone's experience of the underworld as well as by Demeter's life on earth, and the two therefore will be apart for several months each year.

The Demeter/Persephone myth is a very old story, showing how things are psychologically between mother and daughter at the most basic level. In most recent times, the Old Testament stories document the difficulties that the mother archetype suffered in the transition from the earlier goddess-centered cultures to the patriarchal Judeo-Christian mode.

The Book of Genesis is full of old wives' tales of woman trouble. Sarah, Rachel, and Hannah have great difficulties in conceiving. They cannot openly pray to the Mother Goddess, though we know that they did. Eve, Sarah, Rachel, Rebekah, and Moses' unnamed mother suffer the loss and estrangement of their sons. Motherhood is difficult to come by and when it comes to sons, motherhood is marked by painful separation and loss. Stories of mothers and daughters are barely told. Lot's wife looks back, is turned to a pillar of salt, and her daughters end up getting their father drunk and seducing him. Moses' mother sends her daughter Miriam to accompany her baby brother and he later treats her badly.

The Book of Ruth offers a profound insight into the problem of mothers and daughters under the patriarchy where there is a neglect and deterioration of the feminine values and the essentially masculine God is believed to have created all by Himself. It tells the story of Naomi, who with her husband and two sons, is forced to leave the land of Judea because of famine and go to dwell in Canaan where the Mother Goddess is still worshipped. There the two sons marry Canaanite women. Eventually all the men die, again mirroring the famine of the patriarchy in Judea, and Naomi is left with her two Canaanite daughters-in-law. She wishes to return to Judea and urges her daughters-in-law to stay in their own land, saying she herself feels infertile and has no more sons to give them. Oprah stays, but Ruth says, "Whither thou goest, so go I," thereby embracing the new patriarchal value system. So the Hebrew mother, and the Canaanite daughter, together journey to Judea. There, when Naomi's old friends recognize her, and greet her by name, she says, "Don't call me Naomi, I am *Marah*," (later Mary)—bitter, expressing the sense of bitter loss, emptiness and despair of the mother under the patriarchy.

In the cornfields of Boaz, Ruth begins to glean a relative of Naomi. Demeter, you remember, was the corn goddess. Holding up the ear of corn was the symbolic center of her mysteries as they were celebrated at Eleusis. Naomi helps Ruth seduce Boaz into becoming her husband. She tells Ruth to lie with him on the threshing floor at harvest time, recalling the earlier goddess-related fertility rites. Boaz thus is made aware of his desire for Ruth and they do marry and become the parents of Jesse who is the father of David, who, with Bathsheba, gives birth to the wise king, Solomon.

In the story of Ruth and Naomi one sees the rich results of joining the goddess-centered Canaanite religion to the patriarchal Judeo-Christian ways. In terms of the psychology of modern women, the two myths—that of Demeter and Persephone, and Ruth and Naomi—live on within us. One can almost sense the Ruth and Naomi story as a sequel, a picture of what happens between Demeter and Persephone when they have their annual healing reunion.

Chapter Three

HETAIRAE, AMAZONS, AND MEDIUMS

T he opposite of the mother quality is the hetaira, best described by Toni Wolff herself.[1] The hetaira is usually the father's daughter. It is what we become when there is a negative mother complex and one will be anything "not like *her*." Here is a hetaira-type woman describing a mother-type: "Mrs. Pontellier was not a mother-woman. The mother-women seemed to prevail that summer at Grand Isle. It was easy to know them, fluttering about with extended protecting wings when any harm, real or imaginary, threatened their precious brood. They were women who idolized their children, worshipped their husbands, and esteemed it a holy privilege to efface themselves as individuals and grow wings as ministering angels."[2]

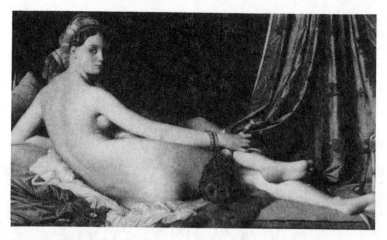

Figure 9. The hetaira woman, with Aphrodite as her goddess. *La Grande Odalisque*, Jean-Auguste Dominique Ingres, 1814, oil on canvas. The Louvre, Paris.

The hetaira woman, with Aphrodite as her Goddess, wakens the individual subjective life in herself and others by conveying a sense of specialness and value, sometimes inspiring others to marvelous achievement. (See figure 9.) Lou-Andreas Salome, the mistress of Nitzsche, Rilke, and perhaps Freud, is a classic of the type. The psychological pitfalls of this quality are, first, that the woman who lives her life as "nothing but anima" is herself unfulfilled, and she may use her considerable power in destructive, deceptive ways. An undeveloped, unconscious hetaira-type woman is often puzzled by her self-deceptive and self-destructive trail of broken relationships, hurt, angry and disillusioned friends and lovers, and her own lack of generativity. The classic tale of the unconscious hetaira-type woman and her relationship to her daughter or her own creativity is Snow White. Here the hetaira mother's envious, spoiling, narcissism repeatedly poisons the development of anything new or creative. Anaïs Nin's diaries[3] exemplify the problems of the hetaira-type woman. The first two diaries have a fresh and creative feminine perspective. Nin is writing to or for her estranged father. The wish to connect to her father is a form of animus energy that carries her for a while and saves her, at first. Similarly, in the well-known fairy tale the mother engages a hunter to kill Snow White, but instead he saves Snow White from an early death, securing for her at least a chance to develop in life. By the end of Volume II, Nin has lost this impetus, and given up her personal style to please Renee Allenby (her first analyst), given away her typewriter and paper to Henry Miller, and given up her home and country to follow Otto Rank (her second analyst) to America to be his secretary. Like Snow White, who works so hard for the seven dwarfs, she repeatedly falls victim to the negative aspects of the hetaira feminine quality. The undeveloped hetaira-type woman chooses men with virulent, unconscious, poisonous fear and hatred of women.

In her later diaries, Nin has fallen into writing cold, unawakened, repetitive, self-serving, narcissistic diatribes against her critics, former friends, and lovers. The hetaira quality in a woman must be engaged by a heroic encounter with her own animus, or she will turn her creations—her daughters—into Snow White fools in glass caskets, endlessly awaiting the kiss of the prince to awaken and free them (see figure 10 on page 38).

The mother and the hetaira are the best known, most evident, and most culturally acceptable archetypes of the feminine. They are opposite poles of the relating or eros quality of the feminine. The mother relates to people in a

Figure 10. The hetaira's daughters, coldly waiting to be awakened. *The Village of the Mermaids*, Paul Delvaux, 1942, oil on panel. Art Institute of Chicago.

collective way, whereas the hetaira relates in an individual way. See figure 11.

On the other axis of Toni Wolff's schema, that of non-personal values, are the amazon and the medium. The amazon quality is present in a woman to the extent that she can function independently and finds pleasure in what she does and accomplishes. Her personality often is formed in her good relationship with her mother, and with the encouragement of her mother's animus and/or her father. These qualities of independence, pride in achievement, and an essentially feminine value system are hard to come by in our culture, although one hopes this is changing.

The ancient Amazons, however, had to sacrifice one of their breasts in order to better aim their arrows. The god-

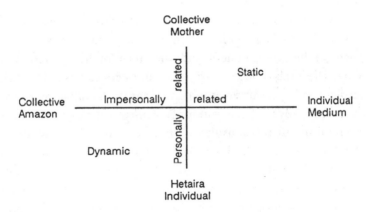

Figure 11. The poles of the feminine archetypes. Adapted from Toni Wolff's schema in her paper, "Structural Forms of the Feminine Psyche," available as a pamphlet at the Kristine Mann Library, 28 E. 39th Street, New York, NY 10016.

desses here are the virgin goddesses Artemis and Athena. Modern women of this type, such as Coco Chanel and Elizabeth Arden, have begun to run successful fashion and cosmetic businesses. I would add Colette, also, because of her tremendous achievement as a woman writer who wrote as a woman. Although she had many husbands and both male and female lovers, her primary identification as a "mother's daughter" remained central throughout her life. For the amazon type of woman, doing predominates, but it always comes of being.

The danger psychologically, for a woman of this type, is being tyrannized by the power animus, adapting his value system, and losing her own essentially feminine standpoint. This power animus can appear in the guise of a man who is a charismatic leader, an idea or belief system, or a company or corporation. Big nurse in *One Flew over the Cuckoo's Nest*[4] is an example of the animus-possessed, undeveloped, unconscious amazon-type woman.

The last of the four types is the medium. "The medial woman," says Toni Wolff, "is immersed in the psychic atmosphere of her environment and the spirit of her period, but above all in the collective, impersonal, unconscious."[5] It is this medial quality in ourselves which brings us in contact with the deep lunar abyss of the feminine. This quality of mediator is essential in our relationships with others, and in our relationships to ideas and thinking. What has been called "woman's thinking," "woman's intuition," "empathic thinking," "diffuse awareness," or "a different voice" is the way of knowing based on this mediumistic quality of the feminine. The individual woman who functions primarily as a mediumistic type must be conscious, and have a strong feminine ego to channel the awesome responsibility for being in contact with these psychic contents. When the ego structure is weak, the mediumistic type of woman can be raped by what she sees and become psychotic, as happens in Par Lagerkvist's novel *The Sybil*.[6] Here, the priests envious of the woman's mediumistic powers arrange her demise. See figure 12 on page 42.

The archetype of the medium is even more important for women in their relationships with themselves, that is, in their own psychological journey toward wholeness. In many ways the Goddess Hestia is a mediumistic soul image for women. She is medium as Demeter is mother. She is a Sybil, a fairy godmother, Baby Yaga, a spinner and a weaver. A woman dreamt that she was in a Mayan land, in a temple of the Moon Virgins and approached her analyst who was a highly intuitive older woman called "the storyteller" in the dream. The dreamer asked her analyst to tell her a story, and the wise old woman replied, "You must become your own storyteller." At that moment, as if by the magic of a fairy godmother, the dreamer saw in her mind's eye exactly the path she needed to follow to become her own medium, or storyteller.

The Goddess Hestia carries much of the archetypal mediumistic quality.[7] Hestia was wooed by both Poseidon and Apollo but swore by Zeus' head to remain a virgin forever. In gratitude to her for preserving the peace of Olympus, Zeus gave her a beautiful privilege instead of a wedding gift: she was to sit in the center of the house to receive the best in offering. The hearth was called her altar, but there were no statues to mark her presence as a personal divinity. The hearth and the hearth-goddess were one. The name Hestia means hearth and is derived from a Sanskrit root *vas* meaning "shining." The element of fire was regarded as pure and divine in its own right and added sanctity to the hearth. In ancient Greece, wherever the fire was burning on a domestic or public hearth or altar, Hestia was present, not as a personal goddess but as a

Figure 12. The archetype of the medium. *The Delphic Sibyl*, Michelangelo. The Sistine Chapel, Vatican City.

divinely emanent power. She seems not to have the anthropo-morphic quality of the other Olympians, but to have arisen in an earlier animistic or preanimistic time from an ancient world of numina and magic.

At Delphi, where Hestia was worshipped, the charcoal heap became the *omphalos* or naval boss, frequently shown in Greek vase paintings which marked the supposed center of the world. This holy object is inscribed with the name of Mother Earth. In classical times, the Pythoness had an attendant priest who induced her trance by burning hemp, laurel, and barley on the hot ashes of the charcoal mound. The mound was sometimes placed on a round three-legged clay table painted red, white and black, which are the Moon's colors.

Ovid explains the round shape of the Temple of Vesta (the Roman name for Hestia): "This is said to have been its shape of old and is based on a sound reason. Vesta is the same as the earth; in the center of them is a perpetual fire; the earth and the hearth are symbols of the home." He goes on to extol its balanced, centered qualities, identifies Vesta as both hearth and sacred flame, and notes that there were no images of Vesta in the Temple, only the undying flame upon the hearth. The hearth or *focus*, he says, is so named because it fosters all things.

The deep psychological significance of the Goddess Vesta for women is suggested by a strange story told by Ovid. In the midst of his descriptions of the many Roman state reli-gious ceremonies and historical events, he tells the following tale:

It chanced that at the festival of Vesta, I was returning by that way which now joins the New Way to the Roman Forum. Hither I saw a matron coming down barefoot:

43

amazed I held my peace and halted. An old woman of the neighborhood perceived me, and bidding me sit down, she addressed me in quavering tones, shaking her head. This ground, where now are the forums, was once occupied by wet swamps: a ditch was drenched with the water that overflowed from the river. That Lake of Curtius, which supports dry altars, is now solid ground, but formerly it was a lake. Where now the processions are wont to defile through the Velabrum to the Circus, there was naught but willows and hollow canes. . . . Yonder God whose name is appropriate to various shapes, had not yet derived it from damming back the river. Here, too, there was a grove overgrown with bulrushes and reeds, and a marsh not to be trodden with booten feet. The pools have receded, and the river confines its water within its banks, and the ground is now dry; but the old custom survives.

Here we sense that there is a special hidden meaning of the Goddess Hestia or Vesta that draws us back to earlier times; times of marshes and water and vegetation; times that still have meaning to the women who walk with their feet in touch with the earth.

Hestia/Vesta's choice to remain virgin, one-in-herself, and not directly related to a man was incorporated into the Roman laws governing the Vestal Virgins. If a Vestal broke her vows of chastity she was stripped of her sacred veil and buried alive. The basis for this particular expiation, I believe, lies in the primary identification of the Goddess Vesta with the Earth. By burying the Vestal alive, the goddess herself becomes the judge of the woman's guilt or innocence and metes out her own punishment. This image is central to the meaning of the quality of "virgin" or one-in-herself to women. The knowledge of her faithfulness to that to which she is pledged comes from the goddess within herself and cannot be judged by manmade laws, or her own animus.

The quality of being true to oneself, exemplified by the Goddess Hestia, is described movingly in Irene de Castillejo's paper on "Soul Images of Women." She defines the soul as "one's essential core" and "the immortal essence that looks out of a baby's eyes."[9] She is speaking of that which each woman knows in herself to be true and which must not be betrayed. Esther Harding describes the psychological meaning of the Virgin as being true to one's own feeling, not to a contract or principle.[10] The psychological necessity of being true to oneself is of particular practical significance for women who are called upon to meet the needs of children, husband, lovers, and others. We are reminded that Hestia was the first of the goddesses, remembered first and last at every meal, and always present in the center of the house. Her primacy and omnipresence point to her necessity and centrality in a woman's spiritual development.

A woman in her aspect as Virgin sacrifices her personal relationship to a man in order to obtain a deeper relationship with her own soul. Ovid explains "Conceive of Vesta as naught but the living flame and you see that no bodies are born of flame. Rightly, therefore, is she a virgin who neither gives nor takes seeds, and she loves companions in her virginity."[11] The Vestals were required to cut off all their hair when they entered Vesta's service, and their shorn tresses were hung on an ancient Lotus tree. By sacrificing their hair, the crowning glory symbolizing their sexual attractiveness to a man, the priestesses gained a deeper feminine wisdom through their worship of Vesta. Homer, in his ode to Hestia, describes her as the goddess "who doth haunt the holy house of King Apollo at Phytho (Delphi) divine, and ever from thy locks sleek unguents trickle down." Hestia the hearth, anointed with the golden oil of sacrifices, is personified as having hair that gives forth wisdom to those who sacrifice to her.

Another story of Ovid's demonstrates the role of sacrifice and purification in feminine psychology. He writes that since he had a daughter he asked when was a propitious time for her to marry: "It was shown to me that June, after the sacred Ides is good for brides . . . the holy wife of the Flamen Dialis spoke thus to me: until the calm Tiber shall have carried down to the sea on its yellow current the filth from the Temple of Illian Vesta, it is not lawful for me to comb down my hair with a toothed comb, or cut my nails with iron, or touch my husband. . . . Thou, too, be in no hurry; thy daughter will better wed when Vesta's fire shall shine on a clean floor."[12] The custom of marrying in June, because it augers well for the bride, survives to this day.

The sacrifices required of the holy Flamenica Dialis until after the purification rites of the Temple of Vesta heighten our sense of the importance of these mysteries which were open only to married women who apparently need them the most, psychologically. From June 9th to June 15th, the storehouse deep in the interior of the temple stood open. Sacred water drawn from a holy spring was contained in vessels made specially with narrow bottoms so that they had to be held on a stand, thereby preventing the sacred water from coming in contact with the profane ground. Ritually made cakes of salt were dissolved in the water. Grain, gathered by the senior Vestal Virgins on certain days in early May, was roasted, pounded, ground and mixed with the specially prepared salt, and offered to Vesta.

In the ritual of the Vestalia, we have several important images. The *solutio* of the salt in the holy water and the ritual mixing of it with grain, reminds us of Jung's writing about the meaning of salt in *Mysterium Coniunctionis*. Salt is the feminine soul: "It represents the feminine principle of Eros, which brings everything into relationship in an almost perfect way . . . its most outstanding properties are bitterness and wisdom."[13] The water is a gift of heaven, and the grain a gift of the earth, each is mixed with the salt, the *anima mundi*. One can only sense the deep psychological meaning of the Vestalia rituals; one cannot elucidate them. There are elements of sacrifice, purification, transformation, and above all, mystery.

At the beginning of the New Year in March, the sacred fire in the Temple of Vesta was rekindled, using a magical wooden fire drill. The fire came from a flat board with a hole in it held by the Vestals, and a phallic pole representing the fire God, Pales, was held upright and twisted by the Pontifex Maximu. This produced friction and a spark that could be ignited only by the breath of a Virgin. In this image lies the deepest meaning of worship of the Goddess Vesta, whose name means shining. A woman who is true to her own feminine soul can be led to the experience of the *Heiros Gammos*, the sacred marriage. The wood is a container of feminine potency, its soul spark is released by the impersonal masculine principle in the ritual act of *coniunctio*.

There is a rebirth here, occurring nine months after the Vestalia mysteries. This synchronicity suggests that the process of introversion and transformation begun in the Vestalia mysteries results in regeneration. In *Mysterium Coniunctionis*, Jung quotes *Ripley's Cantilena* in which the Queen, after being impregnated by the dying barren Old King "unto her chast chamber goes . . . she commands all strangers to be gone, seals

47

up her chamber doore, and lyes alone. Meanwhile she of the Peacocks Flesh did Eate and Dranke the Greene-Lyons Blood."[14]

Jung's amplification of the text makes it clear that the Queen's pregnancy diet consists of the goddess's own attributes; the capacity to grant rebirth symbolized by the peacock's flesh and the blood or *aqua permanens*, the moist soul substance. There are striking and illuminating parallels with the meanings of the grain, salt, and water used in the Vestalia rites. Moreover, in both the Cantilena and the Vestalia, the elements of deep introversion and partaking of one's own feminine nature are essential to the experience of regeneration and rebirth. Surely there is a psychological imperative implicit in these recipes for today's woman in her capacity to mediate the deepest, most profound materials, ideas or works.

Chapter Four

SISTERS AND SHADOWS

When the matriarchal goddess-centered cultures were eclipsed by the patriarchal Yawehists, the feminine aspect of the godhead was suppressed for a very long time. Because of this neglect, rejection, and suppression of feminine values, women who became mothers under the patriarchy were unable to give their children the unconditional love and acceptance that results in whole, healthy, secure, stable, mature human beings. In recent times there has been a return of the goddess, reflected in the culture's wider acceptance of holistic health methods, natural foods, environmental protection, mystical and spiritual experience, and non-linear, cyclical modes of thought and expression.

There has been a revaluing of the feminine, and we have begun a process of Self-acceptance coming from the Feminine

Figure 13. Sister and shadow. From *Women: A Pictorial Archive from Nineteenth-Century Sources*. New York: Dover Publications.

Self. We have begun to know a certain kind of sisterhood that heals and nurtures, and embraces and accepts.

In the Greek myths goddesses and women compete (see figure 13). Someone tosses a golden apple through a window, "for the most beautiful goddess," and Athena, Aphrodite and Hera are at each other's throats. There is Hera's endless jealousy of Zeus's lovers. There is strife between Athena and the girl Arachne about artistry and creativity, and between Aphrodite and her son's lover, Psyche.

In the Old Testament women also compete: two sisters, Rachel and Leah, are both daughters of Laban. There is of course no mother. Jacob falls in love with Rachel, but is tricked into marrying her older, uglier, sister Leah by their father, Laban. The sisters are forced into competition for their husband's love, and children, by their father's manipulation. That is how it has been. Women have suffered in secret isolation, separated from each other, mother and daughter, sister and friend, in a patriarchally defined culture for too long. We have been split into good girl versus bad girl, pretty and ugly, old and young, married and single, rich and poor, and on and on.

These dualities and opposites are shadowed by the ever-present rumor that we are all the same in the dark, in other words, we all have vaginas, though that isn't exactly the word used. For a long time women suffered from that excluding, denigrating, negative definition in silent, separate shame. When the roar of collective suppressed, rejected, neglected feminine wrath broke loose in the late '60s, women began to express some of their goddess-given rage and personal anger, and a cornucopia of women's self-expression flowed forth — art, writing, performance, thought. Women began to read women, listen to women, see women, love women, appreciate, value,

51

nurture and care for women. Sisterhood was recollected. As Monique Wittig wrote in *Les Guerillieres*:

> There was a time when you were not a slave, remember that. You walked alone, full of laughter, you bathed bare-bellied. You say you have lost all recollection of it, remember . . . you say there are no words to describe it, you say it does not exist. But remember. Make an effort to remember. Or, failing that, invent.[1]

We discovered the healing, redeeming joy of finding our own shadows, not the projections of others, but one's *own* unaccepted parts—that which we had habitually cast onto our sisters in the form of negative, competitive projections. Old movies—like *The Women*, *The Big Lie*, *Old Acquaintances*—popular in their day, pit the good girl against the bad, blond against dark-haired, "Betty" against "Veronica." Women were catty, traitorous, and not to be trusted. Rarely were women shown in loyal, loving, nurturing friendship, though I imagine that in real life those relationships must certainly have existed.

Because of the cultural over-valuing of the masculine and undervaluing of the feminine, women were often disappointed and wounded by mothers who couldn't or wouldn't love them, just as they could not love themselves fully. Naturally those young women in an overly compensatory manner, hungrily turned toward their fathers, and later, boyfriends and husbands, for love. Novels of the '50s, *The Group*,[2] *The Best of Everything*,[3] Doris Lessing's five-volume story of Martha Quest[4] detail women's poignant search for love and acceptance from men. Girls grew up expecting to love and marry and live happily ever after, and we certainly tried to do just that. *The Women's Room*,[5] *The Feminine Mystique*,[6] *Memoirs of an Ex-*

Prom Queen,[7] *Diary of a Mad Housewife*[8] are the testimonies of those who tried, really tried to find healing love and self-acceptance in the eyes and arms of a husband's embrace. It didn't work, mostly because we were married to men who themselves had had only wounded mothering and we needed them to be our goddess-mothers. Freud was wrong, we didn't marry our fathers. We married our mothers, and again found only partial acceptance, conditional love, and oceans of tears, disappointment, self-criticism and despair.

It wasn't until the late '60s when men and women began to separate in order to withdraw the projections of the contra-sexual elements in themselves from each other, in order to integrate these elements into themselves, and finally to become more fully whole and human to each other. Romantics among us may wonder whether all these new babies appearing on the streets, carried on the backs and fronts of mothers and fathers may not be the fruits of this new *coniunctio* of men and women.

On the other side, women have also learned that the deep healing comes from their connection with the feminine Self, or the Goddess, or the Shekina, the indwelling feminine side of God. Women have discovered that they can catch glimpses of this feminine Self mirrored in the eyes of other women, friends and sisters. In this sense even our mothers have become our sisters, as in the story of Ruth and Naomi.

Friendships between women have grown. They have always existed, underground, but now they are out in the open and consciously valued. More women know that trusting each other enough to say, "You hurt me when you . . .," or asking "What did you mean by . . .," and saying "I'm angry about . . .," or "I need help with . . .," or "I'm worried about . . .," or "I'm confused, or vulnerable," are all magical incantations to call up the goddess in both her dark and light, negative and positive, elemental and transformative modes. My friend, a Jungian analyst, once made this clear to me by sharing her image of what we did with each other and our patients. She said transference between women is the two of us holding hands and dancing madly around a cauldron. That's not really what she said, but I believe she will understand and accept my misquoting her, and saying instead what I heard. That is part of the process between women and sisters. There is room for merging and blurring the boundaries; now that each of us can hold her own center.

Because women can now begin to accept their underlying sisterhood and connection to the feminine Self, they can also fight it out with a friend and retrieve their own shadow in the process. Women can trust each other and themselves enough to show their needs and vulnerabilities to other women and be mirrored and nourished by each other. I sat with a patient recently who is quite opposite from me in type. She is thinking and sensation. As she was going on and on explaining something about herself, I felt myself becoming an earthy brown potato with little white rootlets and strings gathering her in and embracing her. Her own mother had been an extremely narcissistic self-involved woman physician who (luckily) was never home while the girl was growing up. Suddenly my patient understood herself. She understood what she was trying to work out. She brightened and became quite beautiful and said, "Why, I just remembered. My mother had a dressing table with a three-part mirror that you could move. When I was young, before I even went to school, I would sit surrounded by the three mirrors talking to myself for hours. It felt wonderful. I could understand everything that way." This woman has been so isolated from other women that she has no friends to share herself with. As I, usually the bright, quick, intuitive one, became the dark, drab, sensate potato, she could become for a moment at least, the bright, happy, feeling one.

Sisters become mothers, and mothers become sisters in these relationships and processes. Women mother each other, mirror each other and sister each other, alternately and sometimes both at once. Work on making sisters, and healing wholeness of shadow aspects of oneself can be done on an outer level with friends and sometimes even enemies, and on an inner level when we encounter our feminine shadows in dreams. Often these unacceptable, unlived aspects of personality are just what are needed to solve a problem, fill a gap, or enable us to move forward or backward or up or down. In relating to a shadow sister, use the magical incantation words of need and feeling. Fight it out. Try to get to know her. Be her. Be you. Wholeness will result.

Chapter Five

ANIMUS: LOVER AND TYRANT

Here is an experiment for female readers: try to think of how you feel, or what you think about these essays so far. Take a real stand. This is not for public statement, just for yourself and the purposes of this experiment. How do you really feel about this material so far? All right, now listen carefully. See whether you hear an *other* voice, disagreeing, pointing out, taking an opposite and other view. That is one of the things that Jung meant by animus. He suggests this experiment in the *Visions Seminars*.[1]

When I tried this experiment myself I realized that I was feeling the need for more focused attention. The first few essays are rich experientially, the feelings flow, one can see the variegated, jewel-like beauty of the feminine, and of women's experience, and women; but there is a need for more focus, definition, meaning—something else, the other side.

Figure 14. Animus as lover.

In the myth of Amor and Psyche, when Psyche is charged with the task of stealing the golden fleece, she is aided by the whispering reeds. They tell her that the rams are maddened by the hot noonday sun of solar consciousness beating down on their golden backs. After a long, hot day of ram-like butting heads with each other in masculine aggression and competition, in rage and frustration, crazed by the heat of the sun, the rams lie down and fall asleep. Then Psyche in the cool of the evening can easily gather the golden fleece as it hangs on the twigs and branches that have caught it during the frenetic activity of the day. So we, too, will try to gather some of this golden fleece, but by the light of the moon, and with the help of Psyche's subjective feeling connection and relatedness.

First, a definition of animus: basically, it is the idea that each woman has within herself a contrasexual element, an other, an inner man, partly soul, a masculine side, sometimes a they or a them, a committee, a jury, an editorial board. It is one's inner experience of the masculine other, and sometimes what we expect from men, or the projected outer animus. The animus is formed from our experience of our fathers, of our mother's animus or masculine side, and from the collective unconscious which provides the archetypal dimension. Obvious examples are the stock male characters who appear in dreams, myth, legend and literature — the lover, the rapist, the father, the critic, the bad guy, teacher, boss, or warrior.

As lover, or as positive masculine energy, the animus provides focus. (See figure 14.) As Irene de Castillejo[2] describes it, he holds a lamp allowing us to connect to what we already know on an unconscious level. Emma Jung[3] also sees the animus function as a connector — to word, deed, and meaning. Adrienne Rich speaks of the "Natural Resource" of "the phantom of the man-who-would-understand, the lost

Figure 15. Animus as twin "whose palm bears a lifeline like my own. . ." *Adam and Eve*, Pietro Annigoni, fresco. Convent of San Marco, Florence.

brother, the twin—the comrade/twin whose palm would bear a lifeline like our own."[4] In sum, the animus as lover is at his best as the soulmate, the lost half of oneself restored. (See figure 15.)

The positive animus may appear as father, providing encouragement, protection, principle, containment. He appears in dreams as king, law-giver, father in heaven, even as spirit, wind, sun, or cloud. Or he may be a beloved son, an eternal seeker, a singer, a poet, a creative one, a perfect lover. He lures or inspires. He appears as Adonis, Peter Pan, or David. He may be a hero, a doer, a star who accomplishes things, a cowboy or adventurer. He frees us from personal father, mother, family, and carries us off (see figure 16 on page 62). Or the positive animus may be a wise man who knows, informs, guides, a man who relates to an idea in a subjective way like Moses or Solomon.

Love stories abound with glorious portraits of positive animus-type men, but unfortunately, women most often encounter the animus in his negative aspects, as critic, judge, sadist and evil magician—in short, the bastard. His *modus operandi* is to inform the woman in the most personal and accurate terms that she is no good, worthless, stupid, ugly, unloved, unable and a failure. The animus attack is heard as a negative critical inner voice or attitude, or felt as pain, tension, and rigidity often in the shoulders, back, neck and head.

As tyrant, the father becomes judge. He gives irrelevant general opinions that do violence to the individual. He is unrelentingly critical and negative. He tells us how we should behave and what we should feel. He is concerned with time and history. Like Cronus, the father who devoured his children at birth, he destroys us and our creativity, telling us, "You always . . .," and, "You never. . . ." Caught in this kind of an animus attack, the woman feels like a child or a daughter. She feels bad, pressured, worthless, guilty.

The animus attack of the son or Puer is more subtle. He lures us into fantasy. He is the ghostly lover who takes us away from a real relationship and its difficulties. He is an elusive dreamer, a moony, lazy, boy. He is *Cheri*.[5] (See figure 17 on page 64.) Indolence is characteristic of possession by this animus tyrant. The woman feels heavy and sad as Ishtar mourning Tammuz, or Isis searching for the lost Osiris. She is caught and depressed, paralyzed and unable to function.

The hero animus as tyrant becomes a rapist, a killer, a Nazi, Bluebeard, or Hades. The woman feels like a maiden threatened by invasion, violation, or dismemberment. When the wise man animus becomes tyrannical, we are filled with wishes to be ideal, or we have obsessive shoulds and oughts. The woman sacrifices who she really is in order to fill the

61

Figure 16. Animus as hero. (''Die Erfüllung des Schicksales'' by Edward Burne-Jones, 1888.)

idealized expectations of her animus. A woman caught in the grip of such an animus dreamt[6] that she was a princess who had been given a special gift by her father, the king, and his aide, the magician. It was a magnifying glass that had been affixed to her eye at birth. It had the effect of first magnifying the weak spot of any prospective lover, and secondly of paralyzing any of the hero suitors she looked at. She felt lonely and imprisoned in a high tower.

How does the animus become a tyrant? As Irene de Castillejo[7] points out, the animus is an archetype. As such he is impersonal and inhuman. Unless he is fully and completely informed by the woman, he is apt to be irrelevant and off the mark. This is the most generous interpretation. Barbara Hannah, a wise woman and Jungian analyst and author, is quoted somewhere as saying that in a conversation with her animus she once asked him why he behaved so badly, and he said that he abhors a vacuum, and jumps in whenever the woman isn't there. Mis Hannah has a marvelous paper[8] on this point about "Women's Plots." It is a psychological interpretation of a novel called *Evil Vineyard* by Marie Hay, a typical gothic romance. When one reads the novel one feels the evil power of a man who lures a young woman away from her home and family and keeps her imprisoned in a castle. Barbara Hannah's paper comes as a revelation. She clearly shows how the heroine's lack of ego functioning, of her *not* choosing, *not* expressing, *not* discriminating, was the real villain. Emma Jung[9] explains the tyrannical power of the animus as a spiritual problem. She believed, as I do, that women have a need for spiritual development, and when this need is neglected and culturally denied, there is a resultant tendency to project the Self onto the masculine. That is, the Self is appropriated by the animus. Certainly we have all felt the weight of certain ani-

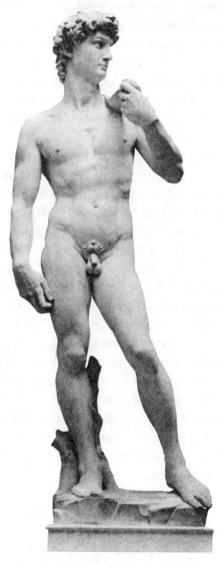

Figure 17. Puer Aeternus—animus as the eternal youth. *David*, by Michelangelo, Florence.

mus judgments of ourselves as though they came straight from God Himself! Marie-Louise von Franz in her wonderful treatise on *Problems of the Feminine in Fairy Tales*[10] describes how hurt feelings unexpressed are always appropriated by the animus and turned into terrible animus attacks, onto others as well as onto ourselves. I always think of this quality of the animus as Oscar the Grouch, a character on "Sesame Street." He lives in a garbage can and grabs all the dirty, negative, ugly stuff he can get. He loves to be nasty. Jung, in the *Visions Seminars*, remarks that the animus is a very hungry fellow, and that everything that falls into the unconscious is possessed by the animus: "he is there with open mouth and catches everything that falls down from the table of consciousness . . . if you let some feeling or reaction get away from you he eats it, becomes strong, and begins to argue."[11]

All these notions of animus energy are correct. Basically, the nature of yin is to reach out and connect, love if you will. While the nature of yang is the opposite, to discriminate and separate. Working out a relationship with one's animus means finding a balance between these two forces in oneself.

The symptoms of an animus attack are feeling caught or possessed, or finding oneself in a rageful spiral, or feeling terribly victimized, or depressed, or feeling a loss of interest in life, or pain or pressure, not being able to breathe, or feeling rigidity, pain or tension in the back, neck, shoulders and head. My image of the "animus-ridden woman" is of the animus riding on the woman's back. Sexual problems, such as not being able to have an orgasm — or coldness — often, involve an animus attack, or animus possession. Obsessive fantasizing and rumination, a feeling of pressure, trying very hard, a certain facial expression, trying lines between the eyes, are all symptoms of the animus attack. Giving advice instead of a human response, feeling cut off from others and life itself are all symptoms of animus possession.

In order to do something about an animus attack, first you must be conscious that this is happening. Second, you must breathe; if possible find a connection to air, earth, fire, or water, something real, basic, and natural, as a countermagic to the irrational hold of by the tyrannical, impersonal, irrational, archetypal possession by the animus. And lastly, you must withdraw the projections from the animus. To do this there must be an active, conscious acceptance of the whole situation. Feel, intuit, think, or sense your way into it. The format is interaction. The animus must be informed of all that you feel or see or think. This is terribly hard to do. Sometimes you have to overcome fear, lack of self-confidence, and/or inertia. It takes courage, but the results are extraordinary.

Chapter Six

ANIMUS DEVELOPMENT

Chapter 5 broadly outlined the animus as lover and tyrant. Now I would like to present an ancient tale that illustrates the vicissitudes in a woman's relationship with her animus. It is the story of Esther told in its entirety in the Book of Esther in the Old Testament. Briefly, the story begins when the king, after several days of drunken banquet with his cronies, demands that his queen appear naked before the men so that he may boast of his possession of her beauty. She refuses. He holds a beauty contest to select a new queen and Esther, a Hebrew woman, is chosen. Her uncle Mordechai tells her of the eunuchs' plot to kill the king. Esther warns the king, and he rewards the uncle by raising him to a position of authority. Mordechai refuses to bow down to anyone, thereby arousing the wrath of the villain Haman, the king's prime minister, who then threatens to kill not only Mordechai, but all the Jews. Esther intercedes with the king. The villain is punished, the uncle rewarded, the people are saved and all live happily ever after. Here is a fairy tale that demonstrates many of the stages and themes of animus development in a woman's individuation process.

First, when we look at the background of this story we have a king, a masculine supreme authority, who summons the queen, commands her to submit to his arbitrary and capricious demands. *She refuses*. This is revolutionary—the basis for the beginning of our story of the separation of masculine and feminine principles. From this ground Esther is given the possibility of individuation, as we all are. That she is a Hebrew woman and promised in marriage already when the king selects her only marks the miraculous nature of this event. She is of the chosen people, those chosen by the Self for individuation.

At the beginning of the story, Esther, whose name is the same as Ishtar, the great Babylonian love Goddess, which means "as beautiful as the moon," is completely contained in the relationship with her animus. She has no father or mother, but has been adopted as a daughter by Mordechai and is being raised to become his wife. She is completely identified with her animus. She does and believes as he tells her. She has the same quality as many women who are at this stage of animus development. They are completely unconscious of the other in themselves, everything is natural and self-evident. They are very much contained in the uroboric connection with the mother.

When Esther is chosen for the beauty contest and separated from Mordechai, she enters the first harem and begins her own process of feminine development. She must keep secret that she is Hebrew. The need for secrecy is an integral part of women's mysteries. In this case Esther is aided in her process by the gift of seven maids. She asked that each of the seven maids serve her on a different day of the week. In that way she could observe the menstrual rituals required of her, and be true to herself without having her secret known, or her process observed. Each maid would see her on only one day and therefore have no overview of her weekly Sabbath observance, nor of her monthly moon cycle ritual ablutions. So the year spent in the harem preparatory to the encounter with the numinous masculine becomes one of turning inward and being true to one's own feminine process. Many women experience such a time in their lives from about age 9 or 10 until they first fall in love.

At the end of this preparatory period, Esther is again chosen, this time by the king. She is selected for further development. Psychologically this is the time that one becomes aware that there *is* an other. The animus, Mordechai, informs her that the king, the ruling masculine principle, is in danger from the eunuchs—those men who are unable to relate to women sexually. Following her animus' instructions, Esther informs the king. This occurrence of the focussed animus-helper Mordechai and Esther saving the king's life later becomes the basis for the transformation of the numinous masculine principle, here the king.

The plot means that the desexualized masculine elements in a woman's psychology will tend to destroy her development and inner marriage, and will prevent her individuation unless she can become conscious of them. This is not an infrequent theme in women's dreams and lives—male homosexuals who must be related to before the process can develop. A woman dreamt that Vietnam war-resisters, veterans who had seen action and then decided to resist, had been made

homosexual by the government, the patriarchy. It was necessary for her to fully understand the meaning of this complicated image in her psyche before she could connect to her own
true soul feelings. Esther does this. She recognizes the plot and
tells the king about it. Almost immediately there is a change
in the king. He gives Haman more authority. Haman
demands that everyone, including Mordechai, bow down to
him. Mordechai, as Esther's animus, refuses because he is
dedicated to a higher authority, the Self.

The masculine principle is becoming more differentiated
for Esther here. This is a very tricky time for a woman
psychologically. She is withdrawing the projection of the
numinous Self from the masculine. There is a potential for
inflation. She feels, "I have made a tremendous step, now I
can handle it *all*." If she is in analysis she is often tempted to
leave it at this point, but very quickly the negative power is
constellated, perhaps by the inflation. She must refuse to bow
down before the negative animus, but this refusal brings with
it the most terrible threat of destruction. Haman tells the king
that a certain unassimilated nation, those that are chosen for
individuation, who follow a unique "outlandish system of
laws," those who are true to themselves, "endanger the stabil-
ity of the realm." The king agrees that they are to be
destroyed, "root and branch," on a certain day, the fourteenth
of Adar, a day chosen by lot or *pur*. The terribleness of the
threat and its fateful nature are emphasized by the choosing of
the day by lot.

Again Mordechai, as Esther's animus, focuses on the
problem immediately and tells her of the threat, but she, as
ego, tries to deny it. Mordechai again informs her that she
must *do* something; she cannot, she says. She cannot appear
before the king unbidden. She will be killed, she says, quoting

70

the animus' law. Psychologically, this is experienced by the woman as a time when she knows what the next step is, but she feels unable to take it.

Then Mordechai as spiritual animus connects her to the transpersonal level in herself. He says:[1]

> Do not suppose that because you are in the King's palace you will be the one Jew to escape. No, if you persist in remaining silent at such at time, relief and deliverance will come to the Jews from another place, but both you and the house of your father will perish. Who knows? Perhaps you have come to the throne for just such a time as this?

Whereupon Esther realizes the nature of her task, and says,

> Go and assemble all the Jews of Susa, and fast for me. Do not eat or drink day or night for three days. For my part I and my maids will keep the same fast, after which I shall go to the King in spite of the law, and if I perish, I perish.

Esther took refuge with the Lord:

> She took off her sumptuous robes and put on sorrowful mourning. Instead of expensive perfumes she covered her head with ashes and dung. She humbled her body severely, and the former scenes of her happiness and elegance were littered with tresses torn from her hair.

These words are an exact description of Ishtar's descent into the underworld in order to rescue her divine son/lover Tammuz.

Esther prays for courage and help. Her prayer speaks from the feminine ego position about the sin of giving over the power of the Self to the false God of animus. A woman in this stage of animus development becomes fully conscious of her history, how the need for the projection came about, and what the dynamic situation really is. She must find out and express what she really feels in order to have a full sense of the plot that threatens to destroy her. Often this involves the breaking of the patriarchal marriage situation wherein the woman is obedient to her husband, not to her Self or to the requirements of her own development.

On the third day, when she had finished praying she took off her suppliant's mourning attire and dressed herself in her full splendour. Radiant as she then appeared, she invoked God who watches over all. . . . Then she took two maids with her. With a delicate air she leaned on one, while the other accompanied her carrying her train. She leaned on the maid's arm as though languidly, but in fact because her body was too weak to support her; the other maid followed her mistress, lifting her robes which swept the ground. Rosy with the full flush of her beauty, her face radiated joy and love; but her heart shrank with fear. Having passed through door after door, she found herself in the presence of the King. He was seated on the royal throne, dressed in all the robes of state, glittering with gold and precious stones — a formidable sight. Raising his face, afire with majesty, he looked upon her, blazing with anger. The queen sank down. She grew faint and the color drained from her face and she leaned her head against the maid who accompanied her.

She fell unconscious — but a moment of Grace occurred.

God changed the King's heart, inducing a milder spirit.
. . . He sprang from his throne in alarm and took her in
his arms until she recovered, comforting her, with sooth-
ing words. "What is the matter, Esther?" he said. "I am
your *Brother*."

This is the first offer of equality.

"Take heart, you will not die; our order only applies to
ordinary people. Come to me." And raising his golden
scepter he laid it on her neck, embraced her and said,
"Speak to me." "My Lord," she said, "you looked to me
like an angel of God, and my heart was moved with fear
of your majesty. For you are a figure of wonder, my lord,
and your face is full of graciousness." But as she spoke she
fell down in a faint.

Again the projection of the Self throws her into unconsciousness, but because she has begun to establish a relationship to
this numinous masculine quality, she is revived and encour-
aged to continue. The story continues:

The king was distressed, and all his attendants tried their
best to revive her. "What is the matter, Queen Esther?"
the king said. "Tell me what you desire; even if it is half
my kingdom, I grant it to you."

Here is the promise of equality and real relationship with the
animus.

Esther accepts the gift and says, "Would the King be
pleased to come with Haman today to the banquet I have
prepared for him?" The king said, "Tell Haman to come
at once, so that Esther may have her wish."

This appearing unbidden before the king—with full consciousness of his numinosity and one's fear—is a great step in a
woman's psychological development. It is a turning point. In
this story Esther then has brought the matter into her own
feminine realm. By her act of reverence and courage she has
gained her own ground. In this context the negative aspects of
the animus are readily transformed. Everything begins to go
well. Things fall into place. Haman, led on by his own inferior feminine side, grandiosely constructs the instruments of
his own demise, the gallows. The animus King becomes conscious of his dependence on the Queen's animus for his very
life. He becomes aware of the need to obey the laws of individuation and relatedness to Self. His negative shadow side is
revealed to him and quickly transformed. Everything comes
out even and right. There is a feast and a banquet and everyone lives happily ever after. The symmetry of the tale, ending
as it began with a feast and a celebration, forms a mandala of
wholeness. The story ends with the words:

> Queen Esther, daughter of Abahail, wrote with *full
> authority* . . . that the Day of Destruction, the fourteenth
> of Adar, would ever after be a day of celebration for all
> her people.[2]

Chapter Seven

THE STAGES
OF ANIMUS
DEVELOPMENT

The animus function connects the feminine ego to the deeper levels of the feminine Self. The development of the animus function brings a transformation in the woman wherein she can assume her *own authority* as a woman. She becomes fully herself and can stand on her own ground, with her *own authority*. In the psychology of women the masculine is experienced in an inner form as animus, and in an outer form as male, and each evokes the other. Successive encounters with the animus, and the ongoing living of life in relationship with others, provides the *way* of individuation for women. It is this continuous, endless encounter with the contrasexual other that provides the *prima materia*, the fire, the energy, and the cauldron for transformation and individuation. The battle of the sexes — or the love story—is always going on in an inner and an outer level and it is necessary to become conscious of it.

I will summarize and outline Neumann's paper "The Psychological Stages of Feminine Development"[1] because it is not readily available. But I strongly recommend that anyone who is seriously interested read this material in conjunction with *The Moon and Matriarchal Consciousness*.[2]

The first stage of feminine development is of maternal uroboric wholeness. There is no separation of the ego from the unconscious. The ego is dependent on the unconscious and contained within it, much as the infant is dependent upon the mother and contained within her. After birth this wholeness is experienced as containment within the "all-embracing, safeguarding power of the group, the clan, or the house. . . . Archetypally this original relationship, namely the total dependence of the ego on the unconscious and of the individual on the whole group is experienced through projection onto the mother, who quite independently of her own individuality impresses the infant or small child as the maternal uroboros and the Great Mother."[3] Structurally, the situation is the same for both sexes, that is, the embryonic and infantile ego are contained in the maternal uroboros. Neumann hypothesizes, and we now know scientifically, that the embryo is male or female from the moment of conception on, and that even the intra-uterine environment is accordingly either male or female. Thus, the baby experiences the mother as either "strange you" or "similar you."[4] And for the boy more clearly, masculine consciousness is born in separating from maternal unconsciousness.

It is necessary to say here that "the totality of the psyche, whose center is the Self, exists in a state of immediate identity with the body, which is the carrier of the psychological pro-

76

cesses."[5] There is a biopsychic difference between the two sexes. Neumann says, "The Self, therefore, as the totality of the personality rightly bears the attributes of the exterior physical sex whose hormonal condition is closely connected with the psychological."[6]

So the boy develops in opposition to the mother through separation and differentiation, becoming evermore objective. The original I-Thou identity is proven false and results in a "tendency to relate only from the distance of the conscious world of logos, as well as in his unwillingness to identify unconsciously with a 'thou.' Thus for boys, 'self-discovery' is essentially bound to the development of consciousness and to the separation of the conscious and unconscious systems, and the ego and isness always appear archetypally as symbolized as masculine . . . He lives the archetypal hero character individually, and only experiences himself after battling with, and overcoming, the dragon, the nature side of the unconscious, which confronts him in the form of the primary relationship."[7]

For the girl, the "original relationship of identity with the mother can (and must) last to a great extent even when she comes to herself as a woman."[8] Thus, the girl's ego development takes place not in *opposition* to, but in *relation* to her unconscious. She feels dependent on it, and nourished by it, and thus naturally turns toward, not away, from unconscious processes. There is the danger of fixation at this level, because the girl can experience herself without ever leaving the possessive circle of the Great Mother archetype. She remains a child-woman, but is not estranged from herself, and enjoys the sense of natural wholeness and completeness, but never becomes a fully developed whole, and human, individual woman. While this natural femininity is held up as a cultural ideal, and one may have to fight to free oneself from it, from an introverted perspective this struggle is *the* interior everlasting task of separation and individuation for women.

Neumann states, "While the relationship to an opposite is an individual and cultural form of relationship, the woman's natural way of relating by identification is derived from the blood bond of pregnancy, that is, from the primary relation to the mother from which this relation essentially stems. . . ." It is typical of the self-conserving phase that the woman remains psychologically and often sociologically in the female group—the mother clan—maintaining a continuity of relationship to the mother group above and the daughter group below. This unity with, and attachment to, the feminine coincides with a splitting off from the masculine and a feeling of alienation toward it.[9] The masculine presence is the mother's animus; any human male is shut out and experienced as a hostile, overpowering and robbing element. The maternal dominance prevents any individual meeting between man and woman.

It is possible for a woman to live in this unborn state, married and with children. Neumann said that to this type everything is "self-evident" and "natural," which often means that she is filled with her own unconscious notions about the character of men in general and of her own particular man, without, as a truly individual reason, ever having experienced men in general, or her man in particular.[10] Thus the masculine side of the uroboros (which is bisexual to be sure) is valued in the matriarchy only as a part of the Great Mother, as her tool, helper, satellite. The male is loved as a child, and as a young boy, and employed as a tool of fertility, but he remains integrated in, and subordinated to, the feminine and is never recognized in his distinctive masculine reality.

78

Neumann's second stage is initiated by the invasion of the paternal uroboros. The woman is seized by an unknown, overwhelming power which she experiences as a formless numinosum. This is always perceived as an experience of the limits of the ego. Later, gradually, consciousness reacts, and a suitable means of adapting to the new archetype is cultivated.

"The development of a divine masculine figure first appears in the matriarchy with the emergence of pluralistic power groups of demonic male characters, such as the Cabiri, the Satyrs, and the Dactyls, whose multiplicity still betrays their anonymity and formless numinousity. These are followed by the figures of the phallic-chthonic gods who, indeed, are still subordinate to the Great Mother, as for example in Greece, Pan, Poseidon, Hades, and the chthonic Zeus. . . ."[11] Typical of these gods are Dionysus, Woton, and Osiris.

The experience of this "invasion by the masculine" is equivalent to an overpowering intoxication, like being seized and laid hold of by a "ravishing penetrator," *not personally related to a concrete man and projected into him, but experienced as a transpersonal numen.*

In dreams and myths the impersonal masculine numinousity may be a god, a cloud, rain, wind, lightning, gold sun, moon, a numinous phallus which penetrates the women in an animal form as a snake, bird, bull, goat or horse. The woman is filled with deathly fear—often symbolized as the death-marriage—she feels herself too small to receive into herself the whole phallus of the godhead.

Clinically, this fear of the masculine invasion is manifested in the classical hysterical neuroses, sexual anxieties, and neurotic symptoms. In analysis there can be an acceptance of the fear, and a surrender to the experience, so that the tremors

79

of anxiety may be transformed into the waves of orgiastic pleasure, and the woman is fructified by the masculine spirit and connected to her own instinctual nature and understands all this with her whole body.

This stage of invasion by the paternal uroboros is essential and hopefully one passes through it and moves on. Fixation at this stage is seen in women who remain fascinated by the Spirit Father, evermore the daughter of the eternal father—prophetess, nun, genius or angel. Or she may personalize the intuitive bond to the spirit father and serve a great man—artist, seer, poet, guru, etc. She is, in short, the animus woman, inflated and "identified with an archetypal feminine figure which widely oversteps her merely human boundaries. . . ."[12] Here the woman loses her connection to earthly reality, to her own humanity, and especially to her own body. Because she is in the thrall of the Spiritual Father, often a black magician, she incurs the enmity of the Great Mother who appears in her negative form as a witch, or, typically, in menstrual and fertility problems.

Another form of fixation at the paternal uroboric level is when the woman identifies with her animus and becomes him. She is estranged from her own nature in an animus possession where she does not know the difference between her Self and her animus. This kind of possession often has tragic results.

It is the task of the masculine hero—appearing in an individual and personal form—to free the captured maiden from the dragon of the paternal uroboros. The masculine hero is both an inner and outer power, and often both appear at once.

The masculine hero usually assumes a personal form. Often the woman falls in love with him; the feminine ego feels unable to separate from the earlier stage by herself and is dependent upon the male hero and in need of help from it. There is a functional relationship between the woman and the animus—he frees her—through word, power, deed, and meaning. He acts as an enlivening impulse and helps her focus on what she wants and how to get it. He gives a more general perspective than does the ego, which is caught up emotionally and is in the middle of things. Outwardly, the third stage is usually the traditional patriarchal marriage, wherein the man's anima is projected onto the woman and the woman's animus is projected onto the man. This form of marriage—the arrangement, I call it—results in the contained and the container, or the House of Cards. The woman is all feminine and the man all masculine. At some point the animus-ridden wife—or the anima-led husband—revolts. There is an accumulation of bitter disillusionment because the mate does not live up to the idealized projected contrasexual element. And there is a crisis in the marriage, or as we have seen culturally, in the patriarchal form of marriage altogether.

Fixation at this level is far more detrimental to a woman than a man because it goes against her feminine Self. She loses touch with matriarchal values altogether and lives as a daughter of the patriarchy. Unlike the daughter of the Spirit Father, inflated, she is instead shrunken, protected, inferior. The opposite loss of soul is true for the man in the patriarchal marriage, but since the cultural values are primarily masculine he is not as reduced as she is. Society as a whole also suffers when it is fixed at this symbiotic form of the patriarchal marriage. If the woman remains faithful to the law or contract of the patriarchal marriage, she is sacrificing her own Self-development.

The fourth phase of psychological development in relation to the animus is marked by confrontation and individuation, and requires the full participation of both partners. It requires that both withdraw their projections from each other, and that they start a new and individual relationship for each of them with their own center—and each other. The woman is urged toward this stage of development by her Self, the man by his anima. For both sexes, the masculine initiates the emergence of consciousness from primary unconsciousness and the *feminine* initiates the completion of consciousness.

Chapter Eight

CREATIVITY AND ACHIEVEMENT

I would like to begin this essay with a parable called *"Life's Gifts."* It was written by Olive Schreiner, a South African feminist, in 1890:

> I saw a woman sleeping. In her sleep she dreamt Life stood before her, and held in each hand a gift—in the one Love, in the other Freedom.
>
> And she said to the woman, "Choose!"
>
> And the woman waited long: and she said, "Freedom!"
>
> And Life, said, "Thou hast well chosen. If thou hadst said, 'Love,' I would have given thee that thou didst ask for; and I would have gone from thee, and returned to thee no more. Now, the day will come when I shall return. In that day I shall bear both gifts in one hand."
>
> I heard the woman laugh in her sleep.[1]

The sense of life forcing us to choose between love and freedom — or in modern terms a career, profession, or a deep involvement with our own creative work — has been with us for years. The diaries and lives of women such as George Sand, Colette, Ruth Benedict, Golda Meir, Virginia Woolf, and many, many others reveal the many layers of this poignant dilemma. Tillie Olsen's book *Silences*[2] is entirely about this problem. The conflict is basically one of separation anxiety. On the extraverted plane we fear the separation from others — mother, father, siblings, collective — that might result from cleaving to one's own self-expression and development. In the inner realm the same anxiety exists in relation to the animus. The inner judging attitude that convinces us of our inferiority and inability takes over and possesses us, holding us fast, and precludes the freedom of relating to an outer love object, whether it be human or creative work that we love.

In 1927 Jung wrote of the plight of the then "modern woman," of her need to develop her own feminine ego as well as her masculine side, and the dangers inherent in such a development:

She develops a kind of rigid intellectuality based on so-called principles, and backs them up with a whole host of arguments which always just miss the mark in the most irritating way, and always inject a little something that is not really there. Unconscious assumptions or opinions are the worst enemy of a woman; they can even grow into a positively demonic passion that exasperates and disgusts men, and does the woman herself the greatest injury by gradually smothering the charm and meaning of her femininity and driving it into background. Such a development naturally ends in a profound psychological dis-union, in short, in a neurosis.[3]

Such a woman would be alone, lonely—both literally and psychologically.

Jung goes on to explain that when such a state of animus possession becomes evident, "there is a special need for the woman to have an intimate relationship with the other sex."[4] He speaks of the plight of single career women and the diffi-culties of a relationship with a married man wherein the single woman sacrifices the security of a home, husband, and chil-dren. On the other hand, married women at that time were beginning to be freed from all that security by the availability of birth control, education and job opportunities. Once the window of opportunity was opened, women could begin to feel the weight, limitation, bonds, and falseness of the tradi-tional marriage as institution wherein they were expected to be all female to the equally constricting all-maleness of their husbands. This containment leads to a death of love, and women began to know this, and long for both a loving human relationship and a loving relationship to work. Jung's essay ends with these words, "It is the function of Eros to unite what Logos has sundered. The woman of today is faced with a tremendous cultural task—perhaps it will be the dawn of a new era."[5]

What *does* dawn on me each time I read this essay, whether in 1967, 1977, or 1987, is my anger at his projection of his somewhat hysterical anima fear that women will become too intellectual, lonely and neurotic if they attempt careers, that they will find only deprivation in relationships with married men, or that they will be invisible or unattrac-tive to single men, and the stunningly blithe expectation and infantile demand that *women* must save the culture. I am equally angered at the truth of Jung's fears then and the persistence of these conflicts today.

Jung himself was surrounded by women who took up the cultural task he mentioned—Esther Harding, Eleanor Bertine, Aneila Jaffee, Marie Jacobi, Marie Louise von Franz—and all these women have addressed the problem of Love or Freedom in their writing. Harding wrote in 1933, "In the beginning of their struggle for independence women were obliged to identify themselves without reservation with their masculine adaptation and for the most part they sacrificed their love life to it completely."[6]

The intense psychological conflicts described by Dr. Harding in the '30s that arise when combining love and work are still with us. In 1968, Matina Horner[7] did a study in which she asked female college students to complete the following story: "After first-term finals, Anne finds herself at the top of her medical school class. And. . . ."

Here are some of the actual stories of these modern women—bright Eastern Ivy League college women—on the eve of the most recent women's movement:

> Anne is a code name for a nonexistent person created by a group of (male) med students. They take turns taking exams and writing papers for her.

Here the students use denial, saying in essence, "It didn't really happen." In another mode a student wrote:

> Anne starts proclaiming her surprise and joy. Her fellow classmates are so disgusted with her behavior that they jump on her in a body and beat her. She is maimed for life.

The typical story, though not quite as bizarre as the above, expressed a great deal of fear of rejection, losing friends, guilt, doubt about one's femininity, despair about success, and anxiety about one's normality in the face of wanting to achieve or succeed.

I searched for a myth or fairy tale that would illuminate these archetypal issues for us. There are several that show aspects of it. The fairy tale of "The Handless Maiden" discussed by Marie-Louise von Franz in *Problems of the Feminine in Fairy Tales*[8] speaks of the sense of inferiority women suffer when not loved by their fathers, and the need for redemption and healing that must precede creative work for such women. The myth of Isis and Osiris illustrates the painstaking construction of a relationship to one's masculine side. The story of how Isis wrested the power of the Sun from the father God Ra is also helpful. But none of these deal with the whole problem, that is, woman's need for creative achievement, her fears of loss of love and relationship, and, most importantly, the paradox that a really good, loving and sexy relationship with another person depends on a woman being whole in herself as a woman and equal as a partner—to both her inner and outer man.

The tale of Amor and Psyche is a love story that illustrates some of the difficulties we experience in achieving wholeness as women. Neumann's analysis of the myth in terms of the development of feminine consciousness is helpful. In addition, I will discuss some of the themes, problems, and difficulties that women have in the area of creativity and achievement.

•   •   •

Once upon a time there lived a king and queen who had three daughters. The two eldest were charming and soon married to kings of neighboring provinces. But the youngest daughter, Psyche, was so strangely and wonderfully fair that soon many of the citizens and multitudes of strangers were drawn to the town to worship her as though she were the Goddess Aphrodite herself. The true Aphrodite grew exceedingly angry at this neglect of her rites and temples and summoned her son Eros. She charged him to "cause the maid Psyche to be consumed with passion for the vilest of men."

In the meantime Psyche herself was miserable because although men marvelled at her divine loveliness, none had come forward to seek her hand in marriage. Her father, seeing her grief, consulted an oracle. He was told:

> On some high crag, O king, set forth the maid,
> In all the pomp of funeral robes arrayed.
> Hope for no bridegroom born of mortal seed,
> But fierce and wild end of the dragon breed.

Heartsick, the king and queen obeyed the oracle and Psyche, arrayed for her ghastly death-marriage, was left trembling and afraid upon the very summit of the crag.

She wept and slept and when she awoke she beheld a grove of lofty trees. In the very heart of the grove, beside a gliding stream, there stood a magnificent palace with a sandalwood roof and columns of gold. Upon entering the palace Psyche was told by bodiless voices that all within it was hers, a gift of some god who watched over her. The voices tended and cared for her, and at night she was visited by her unknown husband Eros who, disobeying his mother Aphrodite, had taken Psyche for his own bride. As time passed, what seemed strange at first became a delight to Psyche, and she looked forward to the nighttime visits of her unknown husband but she did not live happily ever after.

•   •   •

So far the tale has shown us a picture of a beautiful girl married to a man whom she loves blindly. This state of containment expresses psychologically a woman living in a state of blissful unconsciousness of her animus. She is totally identified and possessed by him. She is, in truth, married to a devouring dragon of unconsciousness.

Eros had warned Psyche not to reveal the nature of their relationship to her sisters, but when she becomes pregnant with his child, she is made vulnerable to their questions about who he really is. She needs to know who he is because of the new being growing inside herself.

The shadow sisters, jealous and envious of Psyche's bliss, tell her she is married to the terrible dragon the oracle warned of, and that her child will be a monster if she doesn't kill the dragon. So at the instigation of the shadow elements, Psyche begins to become conscious. She hides an oil lamp and knife beneath her nuptial couch. When Eros has fallen asleep after lovemaking, Psyche lights the lamp and raises the knife to kill him, but when she sees him, she falls madly and deeply in love with Love. She pricks her finger with one of the arrows and, her passion aroused, she casts herself upon him in an ecstasy of love, upsetting the lamp. A drop of burning oil sputters forth and falls upon Eros. He awakens, and seeing his secret betrayed, he flies away and leaves her without a word.

The ideal fantasy situation of the perfect relationship cannot last. The sisters are shadow elements of Psyche herself and stir things up. She is impregnated, her instinctive energies are freed, her creativity is awakened. The sisters' envy represents, I believe, blocked energies seeking a cause. Psyche brings a feminine (vegetable) light to her situation. She is driven toward consciousness and falls truly in love. She begins to know her own feminine nature. At that precise moment she loses the outer man and her relationship is to her own animus.

At just such a point in her own development a woman dreamt, "I had been with my lover for a long time in the Hotel Earle. We left the hotel and I watched as he walked off in his wheat-colored jeans toward the center of Washington Square Park." The "hotel" was a dark place, a secret enacting place for their love affair. The woman who had lived in the Village for many years considered Washington Square to be "her park." It is mandala-shaped and her lover, a hero, and stranger, entered it and moved toward the center—her center, marking the beginning of her relationship to her own heroic animus.

In the myth, however, the wounded Eros goes home to his mother, since the animus is as yet undifferentiated, i.e., a mother's son. This is the aspect of the son-lover which a woman must sacrifice if she is to develop a relationship to her own creative animus. He represents a childish demand to be taken care of that must be given up before a woman can develop her own abilities.

Psyche, bereft and despairing, seeks Eros and contemplates suicide. She meets Pan, who gives her the following advice: "Address Eros, the mightiest of gods, with fervent prayer and win him by tender submission, for he is an amorous and soft-hearted youth." Pan is a god of natural existence and an aspect of the wise and loving spiritual animus. He is Psyche's true mentor, and her process from here on in the story is in accordance with his advice to recognize that her nature is ruled by Eros and to win him she must be true to her feminine Self. Here is the answer to the conflict between Love and Freedom — both, but achieved in our own way.

Eventually Psyche arrives at Aphrodite's palace and Aphrodite sets four tasks before Psyche if she is to be reunited with her lover. The first task is to sort a jumbled heap of millions of seeds of millet, barley, poppy, corn, chick peas and lentils. Psyche is overwhelmed by the task, but aided by tiny ants, she succeeds in sorting the seeds. Faced by millions of possibilities, one must begin sorting.

The feminine diffuse consciousness has a kind of instinctual ordering process represented by hardworking, patient ants. It reminds me of a story that my grandmother often told me: In olden times, in order to tell whether a girl would make a good wife, the future mother-in-law would give the prospective bride heaps of tangled string to unravel. Psychologically, this stage of ego development represents a differentiating, ordering function of the ego — supported by the instinct level. This is the "must" of the feminine ego, rather than the "should" of the animus.

The second task is that Psyche must gather a hank of wool from shining golden rams. Here she is aided by whispering reeds who warn her that during the day the rams are maddened by the fierce heat of the blazing sun, but in the cool of the evening, while they sleep, she can gather their golden fleece from the branches and twigs of the surrounding trees. Symbolically the task is to take possession of the previously overpowering destructive masculine energy. The vegetative, inarticulate, feminine wisdom of the reeds informs her. Like Delilah stealing the masculine power from Samson as he slept, exhausted by feats of lovemaking, the feminine Psyche does not accomplish her task in the light of the noonday sun but in the lunar light of evening. "This feminine wisdom belongs to the 'matriarchal consciousness,' which in its watchful, vegetative, nocturnal way takes what it needs from the killing power of the male solar spirit."[10]

Another example of this process is shown in a story told by a European Jungian analyst about her difficulty in beginning psychoanalytic practice here: She called upon her old family doctor, Dr. Lehman, who said she must go to parties. "Parties," she said, and so she did. When a woman party guest asked if she might see the analyst professionally, the analyst said, "We will see. You will call me on Monday." Monday she sat by the phone and waited, and when the woman called, the analyst said, "Yes, you can come at 3:30 on Wednesday." And then she telephoned Dr. Lehman and said, "Can you come to my house at 3:00 on Wednesday and leave at 3:30?" He agreed, and then the analyst added: "And Mrs. Lehman will come at 4:30!" The typically feminine, veiled but nonetheless heroic deed.

The third task is for Psyche to obtain an urn of water from a rushing mountaintop waterfall. An eagle helps her by taking the pitcher and flying with it to the mountaintop, filling it and returning it to her. Like the blinding destructive brightness of the sun rams, the water of life in this instance is also an overpowering form of masculine energy that Psyche must contain and possess in order to develop. The principle of the eagle, the thinking ego, helps her here.

In the first three tasks Psyche is helped in her development by an instinctual level of consciousness, but in the last task Psyche herself, as ego, must do the deed. She is sent by Aphrodite into the realm of the dead to obtain a certain beauty potion from Persephone. Psyche is warned not to open the vial and not to allow any of the souls of the dead, who approach her and ask for help, into her boat as she descends to the underground realm. The need to say no—the differentiation of one's own needs from others'—is one of the most difficult psychological tasks.

Anaïs Nin, in her second diary,[11] describes giving away her money, her clothes, her typewriter paper and finally even her typewriter to needy friends. She was finally cured of this self-destructive over-mothering in the third diary (1939–1944) by a Jungian woman analyst. The problem is described beautifully in this excerpt from Virginia Woolf:

> I discovered that . . . I should do battle with a certain phantom. And the phantom was a woman, and when I came to know her better I called her after the heroine of a famous poem, "The Angel in the House". . . . She was intensely sympathetic. She was immensely charming. She was utterly unselfish. She excelled in the difficult arts of family life. If there was chicken, she took the leg; if there was a draft, she sat in it. In short, she was so constituted that she never had a mind or a wish of her own, but preferred to sympathize with the minds and wishes of others. Above all, I need not say it—she was pure. . . . And when I came to write, I encountered her with the very first words. The shadow of her wings fell on my page; I heard the rustling of her skirts in the room. She slipped behind me and whispered . . . Be sympathetic; be tender; flatter; deceive; use all the arts and wiles of your sex. Never let anyone guess you have a mind of your own. Above all—be pure. And she made as if to guide my pen. I now record the one act for which I take some credit to myself. . . . I turned upon and caught her by the

throat. I did my best to kill her. My excuse, if I were to be had up in a court of law, would be that I acted in self-defense. Had I not killed her, she would have killed me.[12]

To return to Psyche: she manages to say "no" to the people who beg for her help, and "no" to Persephone who entreats her to stay, but just as she is about to return to Aphrodite with the beauty ointment, she realizes that she will soon see Eros again and cannot resist trying the beauty potion on herself in order to be beautiful for him. Upon opening the vial she falls into a deathlike sleep. Like Sleeping Beauty and Snow White, she goes all unconscious, but Eros, by now more developed (by Psyche's labor) goes to his father Zeus and obtains permission to awaken Psyche; and Aphrodite, because she is, after all, a love Goddess, understands and forgives. I think I once read an interview with Doris Lessing in which she said she never knew a male writer who would sacrifice his career for a love affair, and she never knew a female writer who wouldn't.

The best for last: when Psyche, reunited with her lover Eros, finally gives birth, it is to a divine daughter called Pleasure.

A patient of mine, after many years of struggle to find her own career, was finally successful. She was primarily a mother type, and became a small grants giver to grass roots projects for a well-endowed foundation. She dreamt that when faced by the slow-moving elevators of the large corporate office building in which she worked, she gleefully devised a way for people to play basketball as they waited.

To explicate the problem of doing in a feminine way I would like to use some words from Anaïs Nin describing what she feels is "woman's creativity." These passages grew

94

out of an evening spent with Henry Miller, Laurence Durrell and his wife, Nancy:

> My feeling for woman's inarticulateness is reawakened by Nancy's stutterings and stumbling. . . . "Shut up," says Larry to Nancy. She looks at me strangely, as if expecting me to defend her, explain her.

Nin on the issue of objectivity:

> Look at the birth story. It varies very little in its polished form from the way I told it in the diary immediately after it happened. . . . Objectivity may bring a more rounded picture, but the absence of it, empathy, feeling with it, immersion in it, may bring some kind of connection with it.

> As to all that nonsense Henry and Larry talked about, the necessity of "I am God" in order to create . . . woman never had direct communication with God anyway, but only through man, the priest. But what neither Larry nor Henry understands is that woman's creation far from being like man's must be exactly like her creation of children, that is it must come out of her own blood, englobed by her womb, nourished with her own milk. It must be a human creation, of flesh, it must be different from man's abstractions. As to this "I am God," which makes creation an act of solitude and pride, this image of God alone making sky, earth, sea, it is this image which has confused woman. . . . Woman does not forget she needs the fecundator, she does not forget that everything that is born of her is planted in her. If she forgets this she is lost.[13]

Figure 18. Doña Rosa, potter of the earth, Oaxaca, Mexico.

Figure 19. The Spinner. ''The mystery of giving birth is basically associated with the idea of spinning and weaving and complicated feminine activities. . .''—Marie-Louise von Franz. Photograph is ''Spain, Spinner, 1951,'' by W. Eugene Smith. ©1978 SherArt Images, New York.

Achievement is the work of the ego, and creation is the work of the Self; both, for women, are feminine in timing, process, methods, and style. (See figure 18 on page 96.) Women's work is often individual and original, since women have not been socialized to be team players or members of the club, or gentlemen. The creative process, directed by the feminine Self, the lifegiver, matrix, and nurturing one, draws on both the transformative and the mothering aspect of the feminine. (See figure 19 on page 97.) Creation has strong parallels to conception, gestation, birth and nursing in the physical world; while achievement has as its base the sexual relationship to the animus that results in a strong, well-developed feminine ego.

The story of Eros and Psyche outlines many of these problems, but there is really not yet a happy ending. We are left at the end as we are at the beginning with the problem of how to live one's life as a woman out of the feminine ego/Self axis, with the help of the animus. But if the animus directs the show we're lost, or if *he* does all the work, it's no good and becomes self-destructive. Finding the way to work out of the feminine ego/Self axis is *the* journey of individuation for women.

Chapter Nine

WITCH AND
WISDOM

The witch lives alone at the edge of town, or deep in the forest, in the desert, or at the edge of the Red Sea. She is ugly or beautiful. She combs her long, tangled hair with a claw. She has painted breasts that contain no milk, hairy legs, and the foot of a goat, an ass, a chicken, or an owl.

Witches are creatures of the night encountered in dark places—at crossroads, under archways, doorways or bridges, in latrines and wells. Witches are associated with the moon, the raven, bats, hounds, frogs, and toads. Witches fly about at night by their own winged power, or on broomsticks, or like Baba Yaga in a mortar with a pestle to row with. (See figure 20 on page 100.)

The witch is the despised and rejected feminine archetype. She is not the merciful mother of God, no indeed; she is the devouring child-killing dark Kali, skulls hung around her

Figure 20. Witches fly through the night. *Bat-woman*, Albert Penot, 1890, oils.

neck, bones making a hedge around her house. She is not the bountiful, creative, lush green of nature, but the dark, cruel, senseless destructive aspect. She is not the loving, compassionate, succoring companion of man. No. She is essentially alone. Herself. Sexually voracious, a vixen, a Circe, alluring and again ultimately devouring and death-dealing.

Mother Holle, or Hulda the Teutonic demon mother witch who gobbles up children and babies, appears as the love Goddess Venus in the following 15th century Hebrew-Yiddish love recipe:

> Secure an egg laid on a Thursday by a jet black hen which has never laid an egg before, and on the same day, after sunset, bury it at a crossroads. Leave it there three days, then dig it up after sunset, sell it and purchase with the proceeds a mirror, which you must bury in the same spot in the evening in the name of Venus, and say, "All that you have in life Mother Hulda, give to Venus." Sleep on that spot three nights, and then remove the mirror, and whoever looks into it will love you![1]

The devouring mother becomes the irresistible seductress. Or perhaps one could use this recipe to secure Self-love. Here is another picture of a witch at her work as described in the Zohar:

> She adorns herself with many ornaments like a despicable harlot, and takes up her position at the crossroads to seduce the sons of man. When a fool approaches her, she grabs him, kisses him, and pours him wine of dregs of viper's gall. As soon as he drinks it, he goes astray after her. When she sees that he has gone astray after her from the path of truth, she divests herself of all ornaments

Figure 21. The witch in the mirror. *The Sin*, Franz von Stuck, 1893.

which she put on for that fool. Her ornaments for the seduction of man are: her hair is long and red like the rose, her cheeks are white and red, from her ears hang six ornaments. Egyptian chords and all the ornaments of the Land of the East hang from her nape. Her mouth is set like a narrow door comely in its decor, her tongue is sharp like a sword, her words are smooth like oil, her lips are red like a rose and sweetened by all the sweetness of the world. She is dressed in scarlet, and adorned with forty ornaments less one. Yon fool goes astray after her and drinks from the cup of wine and commits with her fornications and strays after her. What does she thereupon do? She leaves him asleep on the couch, flies up to heaven, denounces him, takes her leave and descends. That fool awakens and deems he can make sport with her as before, but she removes her ornaments and . . . stands before him clothed in garments of flaming fire, inspiring terror and making body and soul tremble, full of frightening eyes, in her hand a drawn sword dripping bitter drops. And she kills that fool and casts him into Gehenna.[2]

And she stirs her cauldron, brews her brew, and spins her web. What witches do is largely circular, cyclical like the moon. They spin and weave, and brew and cook; and dream and scheme, and cast spells, enchant, tell fortunes, pose riddles, set tasks, read dreams and prophesy.

A witch can render you unconscious into deathlike sleep for a hundred years. (See figure 21.) A witch can make a baby laugh in its sleep, tangle its hair, or strangle it. A witch can turn a man into a pig as Circe did to her lovers, or hold you prisoner in a tower or a glass coffin until your hero comes to free you.

We are all pretty witchy in our ways, since all that is rejected and despised in the feminine archetype is suppressed and repressed in us — it becomes shadow and worse.

Lilith,[3] who was present at creation, has a long and glorious career as a witch, representing the neglected, rejected aspects of the Goddess in both her aspects — as seductress, as well as devouring mother. The only reference to Lilith by name in the Old Testament occurs when Isaiah, in describing Yahweh's day of vengeance when the land will be turned into a desolate wilderness, says:

> The wild cat shall meet with the jackals
> and the satyr shall cry to his fellow.
> Yea, Lilith shall repose there
> and be to her a place of rest.
>
> (Isaiah 34:14)

Lilith was Adam's first wife; her origins are described in Genesis 1:27: "In the image of God he created him, male and female he created them." Lilith insisted on equality with Adam — including not lying beneath him in sexual intercourse — basing her claim on their both having been created from dust. When Lilith saw that Adam was determined to overpower her, she uttered the ineffable magic name of God, rose into the air, and flew away to the edge of the Red Sea where she engaged in unbridled promiscuity with lascivious demons and gave birth to "Lilim" at the rate of more than one hundred a day.

Adam complained of her desertion to God, who immediately sent forth three angels to bring Lilith back. "Return to Adam," they demanded, "or we will kill you." According to the Aleph Bet Ben Sira, 15th century, Lilith replied, "How can I die when the Holy One has ordered me to take charge of all newborn babies, boys until the eighth day of life [when they are circumcised and named] and girls until the twentieth day? Nonetheless, if ever I see your three names, or likenesses, displayed in a magic circle amulet above a newborn child, I promise to spare it." To this they agreed; but God punished Lilith by making one hundred of her demon children perish daily.

Lilith dwelt alone in the wilderness, until Adam and Eve separated following their awareness of Cain's sin. Adam fasted, refrained from intercourse with Eve, and wore a belt of rough fig twigs around his naked body. But when Lilith visited him at night, he was unable to control his nocturnal emission, and she satisfied herself with him and brought forth the plagues of mankind.

In fact, ever after Lilith visited the beds of men and women who slept alone, rousing their desire and coupling with them, causing orgasm and ecstasy. And even when a man wishes to engage in lawful sexual intercourse with his wife, it is said, "Lilith is always present in the bedlinen of man and wife when they copulate, in order to take hold of the sparks of the drops of semen which are lost." In unholy forms of intercourse—that is, when a man couples with his wife by candlelight, or with his wife naked, or at a time when he is forbidden to have intercourse with her—Lilith is present and has dominion over the children who issue from such unions.

Lilith is said to have married Tobal Cain and to have come to Solomon as the Queen of Sheba, her hairy legs betraying her demonic state, and as the two harlots who both claimed the child. In the Song of Songs, I believe it is she who says:

105

I am black but lovely,
daughters of Jerusalem
Like the tents of Kedar,
Like the pavilions of Salmah.
Take no notice of my swarthiness
It is the sun that has burnt me.
My mother's sons turned their anger on me,
They made me look after their vineyards.
Had I only looked after my own!

In another legend Elijah encountered Lilith on her way to murder a child of a daughter of Eve. Said Elijah, "May you be interdicted from this by the Name of the Lord, blessed be He! Be silent as a stone." Lilith replied, "O Lord release me and I swear by the name of God to forsake my evil ways, and as long as I see or hear my *own* names I shall have no power to do evil or to injure. I swear to disclose my true names to you. And these are my names: Lilith, Abiti, Abiga, Amrusu, Hakash, Odem, Ik, Pudu, Ayil, Matruta, Avgu, Katah, Kali, Batuh, Paritasha. From all those who know these names and use them I promise to run away."[4]

There are many other legends about Lilith: She is the wife of Samael, the Other God or devil; she is called the Shekina, the highest form of feminine spirit in the Kabbalah, and even became God's consort at the time of the destruction of the temple. The identity of the opposites in Lilith and the Matronit, the feminine aspect of God, is apparent. Lilith is ever present for us as women, and we must be conscious of her in us in order to avoid falling into evil ways, or danger.

Specifically, if we ignore Lilith in her many witchy guises, that is, if we are not conscious of her names, she will kill our babies; i.e., our creativity, our impulse toward growth and development. In short, she will strangle that newborn creative impulse that is dearest to us. Similarly she will come between us and our lover, stealing his desire and inseminating creative energies away from us. This can happen outwardly, ruining a relationship with a man, or inwardly between a woman and her animus.

If a woman is identified with Lilith, she will destroy newborn elements within and without, she will live in the wilderness and feel ostracized, black, rejected and vengeful. She will tempt and seduce men she has no feeling for out of a power motive. And her sense of isolation and desolation will increase daily.

Lilith is pictured on Babylonian bowls dating from A.D. 600 bound in chains and with the following incantation:

> Bound is the bewitching Lilith with a peg of iron in her nose; bound is the bewitching Lilith with pinchers of iron in her mouth; bound is the bewitching Lilith . . . with a chain of iron on her neck; bound is the bewitching Lilith with fetters of iron on her hands; bound is the bewitching Lilith with stocks of stone on her feet.[5]

Complete suppression is a primitive way of dealing with a goddess who has promised to run away and do no harm if only her names are known or written. Similarly, many of the Babylonian bowls were inscribed with divorce writs addressed to Lilith:

> Be informed herewith that Rabbi Joshua bar Perahia has sent the ban against you. A divorce-writ has come down to us from heaven. . . . Thou Lilith, Hag and Snatcher, be under the ban. . . . A divorce-writ has come for you across the sea. . . . Hear it and depart. . . . You shall not

Figure 22. Becoming wicca: we can perform private rituals to become ''wise women.'' *Steinfrau*, photography by Ine Guckert, Forstinning, W. Germany.

again appear . . . either in a dream by night or in slumber by day, because you are sealed with the signet of El Shaddai, and with the signet of the house of Joshua bar Perahia and by the Seven who are before him. . . . Thou Lilith . . . Hag and Snatcher, I adjure you by the Strong One of Abraham, by the Rock of Isaac, by the Shaddai of Jacob, by Yahweh his name . . . by Yahweh his memorial . . . turn away from [this house] . . . your divorce and separation . . . sent through holy angels . . . the Hosts of fire in the spheres, the Chariots of El Panim before him standing, the Beasts worshipping in the fire of his throne and in the water. . . . Amen, Amen, Selah, Halleluyah![6]

Such methods have never worked, and certainly do not work psychologically on the individual level. In fact, the way we deal with the witch in ourselves is just the opposite. We must, as the Talmudic myths say, be conscious of the names of the three angels sent by God—that is, of our connection to the Self as well as to the fourteen names of Lilith, or the many facets and details of our Lilith nature.

This last section should be called "Becoming Wicca (wise women): How to Do It." Because these witch qualities are the shadow, they are close to the transpersonal. It is well to indulge a witchy mood. That means be alone—probably in your own house and your own special place in it. (See figure 22.) Brood and stir and pay attention to your process (remembering the three angels). Sew, crochet, embroider, cook, paint, write, make music, dance, read, dream, scheme, do your nails. Spend hours bathing, oiling and painting and perfuming yourself. Marie-Louise von Franz says that "the mystery of giving birth is basically associated with the idea of spinning and weaving and complicated feminine activities consisting in bringing together natural elements in a certain order."[7] In these activities one gives birth to fantasies, webs and intrigues in which we can read our real motives. A Babylonian manuscript offers these safeguards against Lilith: Place a needle close to the wick of a lamp, or place a measure used to measure wheat in the room of the woman who is to be protected from Lilith. The sewing, weaving, stirring or containing activities seem to draw Lilith into the room, then if we are properly receptive, we can see her. Marie-Louise von Franz in *Shadow and Evil in Fairy Tales* and in *Problems of the Feminine in Fairy Tales* tells the story of the little girl who is sent to get fire from Baba Yaga. The witch encourages the girl to ask her questions about her attributes, but at a certain point she warns one must allow the mystery to remain unopened.[8] You will know that point when you come to it in yourself, I think. That is just a small witch-like warning. The important part of the recipe is to "brood and stir and pay attention."

Most often, I think, a woman finds in her witch's brew her own needs for love, relatedness, dependency, sex. She finds these needs at an unacceptable level—too needy—too dependent—too physical—whatever has been despised and rejected in her own personal experience. These are the unexpressable needs and feelings that become the witch, the child killer and the unrelated power seeker.

If we can accept these needs in ourselves, and if we can accept our rejected and vengeful feelings, we are well on the way toward wholeness. On a more practical level, by being aware of motives, needs and feelings, and accepting them, the witch-like powers are far more effective.

Try a Lilith recipe of bathing, painting and perfuming yourself in preparation for meeting a certain man. Pay attention to your fantasies so you know what you want from him.

And then when you are with him, look in his eyes and think of what you want. (It is very important to be sure that you really want it because this works!) It's not what you do—not ego—this is all love magic—a matter of accepting your Lilith nature, your needs, your shadow side.[9]

Rivkah Kluger, in a brilliant essay about the Queen of Sheba, tells how Solomon had a glass floor built into his throne room so that when the Lilith, disguised as the Queen of Sheba, approached him she would think that his throne sat in water. In order to cross the water and approach him she would lift her skirts, thereby revealing her hairy legs, an unmistakable sign of her demonic, witch-like nature.[10] Because the Queen of Sheba's "problem" is made conscious, she is able to reach a higher level of development and come to her own deepest sources of feminine wisdom. Similarly, we are told that Baba Yaga rides around in a mortar and uses a pestle to row. According to Marie-Louise von Franz, this symbolizes a grinding down to the essentials—to the *prima materia*.[11] It is a realization of the shadow which goes so deep that we can say nothing more about anything. It is the turning point. The ego in its negative aspect has been pulverized, and has to give in to greater powers. (See figure 23 on page 112).

On an individual level, each woman carries the neglected, rejected, homeless, and exiled aspects of the feminine in her shadow side, but on a wider cultural, deeper archetypal and higher transpersonal plane, the feminine side of God must be redeemed in order to bring healing, wholeness, and balance to the planet and humankind.

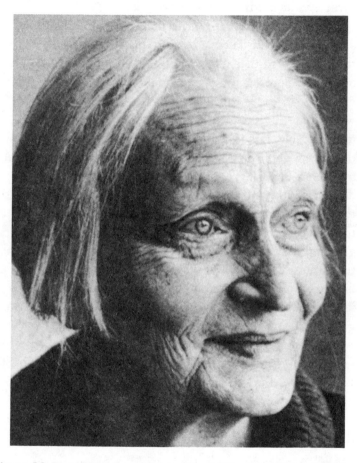

Figure 23. Irina Tweedie, whose spiritual diary is *The Chasm of Fire*, writes: ''The path of love is like a bridge of hair across a chasm of fire.'' Photo of Irina Tweedie by John Moore. Used by permission.

Epilogue

I have been thinking a lot about time and aging lately: the hag and the crone and the wise old woman. A dozen years ago, when I wrote about becoming Wicca, I seem to have thought about that as the end. But here and now, it seems only midway to me.

I have a close friend who has been for me, variously, mother, sister and daughter. We met more than twenty years ago when my daughter was born and my friend was a nineteen-year-old moving into the studio apartment next door to begin her junior year at New York University. She is now a successful artist who paints huge environmental works, runs an art investment business, and has two little daughters of her own under the age of four. In some ways her life is very different than mine was when my children were small. She thinks love affairs between people who are geographically separated should be conducted by FAX machines because she values their direct sequential communication over the thickly braided ambiguous vicissitudes of letters trusted to the postal systems of distant lands. But recently I asked her, "How are you?" And she replied, "There's too much life." I knew just exactly how she felt. Women, both ancient and modern, are by nature attached to a moon cycle, to people, to work and to Self. We are embedded in life. There is endless process.

I know now why Penelope wove by day, and unravelled by night while her husband Ulysses roamed the world. They say it was to keep her suitors away; but I know it was her own—*our* own—endless process that occupied her.

Originally, the title *Weaving Woman* was meant as a double entendre. I thought it reflected both process and *materia*, the concept of woman. The collection could have been called simply *Feminine*, because the one word itself says it all, and it *is* all process. There is no such thing as a completed definition of woman. A woman is a weaving, woven, unravelling, *moving* female energy and experience.

Endnotes

Chapter One

1. These are the words of a noble Abyssinian woman spoken to Frobenius, an anthropologist, in 1899 and quoted by C.G. Jung and C. Kerenyi in their book *Essays on a Science of Mythology*, Bollingen Series, Vol. 22 (Princeton, NJ: Princeton University Press, 1963), p. 101. Used by permission.
2. From personal correspondence. Used by permission of the author.
3. See, for example, *The Book of Lilith*, by Barbara Black Koltuv (York Beach, ME: Nicolas-Hays, 1986).
4. This dream, and all the dreams described in these essays, are used with the express consent of the dreamers, who wish to remain anonymous.
5. These descriptions appear on pages 72 and 184 of *The Early Diary of Anaïs Nin, Vol. II, 1920–33* (San Diego: Harcourt, Brace, Jovanovich, 1983.)
6. One form of kohl is made of finely ground stone. Another, used by Bedouin women, is made from the carbon smoke deposits of olive oil burnt in lamps.
7. I have used the Jerusalem Bible (New York: Doubleday, 1961) for all biblical quotes throughout this book.
8. M. Esther Harding, *Women's Mysteries* (New York: Harper & Row, 1976), p. 103.
9. Irene Claremont de Castillejo, *Knowing Woman* (New York: Harper & Row, 1974), pp. 165–182.

10. If you can grab hold of the horn of the moon with your left hand, it is waxing. If you can only grab onto it with your right hand it is waning.

11. For the full story of the power of the menstruating women throughout two thousand years of history, see Hannah Koltuv's unpublished Baccalaureate Honors Thesis, "Forbidden Lust: Menstrual Taboos in the Jewish Tradition," Amherst College, 1988.

12. Charlotte Painter, "The Story of a Pregnancy," in *Who Made the Lamb* (San Francisco: Creative Arts Books, 1988).

13. Padraic Colum, *Myths of the World* (New York: Grossett and Dunlap, 1934), p. 35.

14. Colum, *Myths of the World*, p. 36.

15. Sylvia Plath, "Ode to Lesbos," in *Ariel* (New York: Harper & Row, 1961).

Chapter Two

1. Toni Wolff's "Structural Forms of the Feminine Psyche" is available in English as a pamphlet at the Kristine Mann Library, 28 E. 39th Street, New York, NY 10016.

2. C.G. Jung and C. Kerenyi, *Essays on a Science of Mythology*, Bollingen Series, Vol. 22 (Princeton, NJ: Princeton University Press, 1963), p. 162. Used by permission.

3. Adrienne Rich, *Of Woman Born*, in the essay "Mothers and Daughters" (New York: Norton, 1986), p. 219.

4. Rich, *Of Woman Born*, p. 226.

5. Philip Zabriskie, "Goddesses in Our Midst," in *Quadrant* No. 17 (New York: C.G. Jung Foundation, Fall, 1974), pp. 34–45.

6. Erich Neumann, *The Great Mother*, Bollingen Series, Vol. 47 (Princeton, NJ: Princeton University Press, 1964), p. 25.

Chapter Three

1. Toni Wolff, "Structural Forms of the Feminine Psyche," available as a pamphlet at the Kristine Mann Library, 28 E. 39th Street, New York, NY 10016.

2. Kate Chopin, *The Awakening* (New York: Avon, 1972), p. 8.

3. Anaïs Nin, *The Diary of Anaïs Nin*, Vols. 1–7 (New York: Harcourt, Brace, Jovanovich, 1976–1986).

4. Ken Kesey, *One Flew Over the Cuckoo's Nest* (New York: Penguin, 1977).

5. Wolff, "Structural Forms of the Feminine Psyche," p. 9.

6. Par Lagerkvist, *The Sybil* (New York: Random House, 1963).

7. Barbara Black Koltuv, "Hestia," in *Quadrant* Vol. 10, No. 2 (New York: C.G. Jung Foundation, Winter, 1977), pp. 58–63.

8. Ovid, *Fasti*, Vol. I, trans. James G. Frazer (Cambridge: Harvard University Press, 1951), p. 327.

9. Irene Claremont de Castillejo, "Soul Images of Women," in *Knowing Woman* (New York: Harper & Row, 1974).

10. M. Esther Harding, *Woman's Mysteries* (New York: Harper & Row, 1971).

11. Ovid, *Fasti*, Vol. I, p. 317.

12. Ovid, *Fasti*, Vol. I, p. 315.

13. C.G. Jung, *Mysterium Coniunctionis*, Collected Works of C.G. Jung, Vol. 14, Bollingen Series, Vol. 20 (Princeton, NJ: Princeton University Press, 1970), p. 241.

14. Jung, *Mysterium Coniunctionis*, p. 285.

Chapter Four

1. Monique Wittig, *Les Guerillieres* (Boston: Beacon, 1985), p. 89.

2. Mary McCarthy, *The Group* (New York: Harcourt, Brace, Jovanovich, 1963).

3. Rona Jaffee, *The Best of Everything*. Now out of print, but available as a movie.

4. Doris Lessing, *The Children of Violence* (New York: Plume, 1970).

5. Marilyn French, *The Women's Room* (New York: Summit, 1977).

6. Betty Friedan, *The Feminine Mystique* (New York: Norton, 1983).

7. Alix Kates Shulman, *Memoirs of an Ex-Prom Queen* (Chicago: Academy of Chicago Publishers, 1985).

8. Sue Kaufmann, *Diary of a Mad Housewife*. Now out of print, but available as a movie.

Chapter Five

1. C.G. Jung, *The Visions Seminars* Vol II. (Zurich: Spring Publications, 1976), pp. 497–98.
2. Irene Claremont de Castillejo, *Knowing Woman* (New York: Harper & Row, 1974).
3. Emma Jung, *Animus & Anima*, C.F. Baynes and H. Nagel, trans. (New York: Spring Publications, 1985).
4. Adrienne Rich, lines from "Natural Resources" in *The Dream of a Common Language* (New York: Norton, 1978), p. 63.
5. Colette, *Cheri*, (New York: Ballantine, 1982).
6. This dream and all the dreams mentioned in this book are used with the express consent of the dreamers, who wish to remain anonymous.
7. Castillejo, *Knowing Woman*.
8. Barbara Hannah, "The Problem of Women's Plots in *The Evil Vineyard*" (The Guild of Pastoral Psychology, No. 51, February 1948.)
9. Emma Jung, *Animus & Anima*.
10. Marie-Louise von Franz, *Problems of the Feminine in Fairy Tales* (New York: Spring Publications, 1972), p. 27.
11. C.G. Jung, *The Visions Seminars* Vol. I (Zurich: Spring Publications, 1976), p. 6.

Chapter Six

1. The entire tale is told in The Book of Esther in the Old Testament. I used the *Jerusalem Bible* (New York: Doubleday, 1961) for the particular wording of the story as it unfolds here.
2. Italics are mine.

Chapter Seven

1. Erich Neumann, "Psychological Stages of Feminine Development" (Analytical Psychology Club of New York, Spring, 1959). This may be read in typescript at the Kristine Mann Library, 28 E. 39th Street, New York, NY 10016.
2. Erich Neumann, "The Moon and Matriarchal Consciousness" in *Fathers and Mothers* (Zurich: Spring Publications, 1973), pp. 40–63.
3. Neumann, "Psychological Stages of Feminine Development," p. 63.
4. Ibid., p. 64.
5. Ibid., p. 65.
6. Ibid., p. 65.
7. Ibid., p. 66.
8. Ibid., p. 67.
9. Ibid., pp. 67, 68.
10. Ibid., p. 69.
11. Ibid., p. 71.
12. Ibid., p. 73.

Chapter Eight

1. Olive Shreiner, "Life's Gifts" in *Dreams* (Boston: Roberts Brothers, 1894).
2. Tillie Olsen, *Silences* (New York: Dell, 1979).
3. C.G. Jung, "Woman in Europe" in *Civilization in Transition, Collected Works of C.G. Jung*, Vol. 10, Bollingen Series, Vol. 20 (Princeton, NJ: Princeton University Press, 1970), p. 119.
4. Jung, "Woman in Europe," p. 119.
5. Jung, "Woman in Europe," p. 133.
6. M. Esther Harding, *The Way of All Women* (New York: Putnam, 1970), p. 69.
7. Matina S. Horner, "A Psychological Barrier to Achievement in Women—the Motive to Avoid Success" (Symposium presentation at the Midwestern Psychological Association, May 1968, Chicago), p. 11.
8. Marie-Louise von Franz, *Problems of the Feminine in Fairy Tales* (New York: Spring Publications, 1972).
9. Erich Neumann, *Amor and Psyche*, Bollingen Series, Vol. 54 (Princeton, NJ: Princeton University Press, 1956).
10. Neumann, *Amor and Psyche*, p. 101.
11. Anaïs Nin, *The Diary of Anaïs Nin 1934–1939*, Vol. II (San Diego: Harcourt, Brace, Jovanovich, 1983).
12. Virginia Woolf, from "Professions for Women," in *The Death of the Moth and Other Essays* (San Diego: Harcourt, Brace, Jovanovich, 1974), p. AU.
13. Anaïs Nin, *The Diary of Anaïs Nin 1939–1944*, Vol. III (San Diego: Harcourt, Brace, Jovanovich, 1985), pp. 208–295.

Chapter Nine

1. Joshua Trachtenberg, *Jewish Magic & Superstition* (New York: Atheneum, 1979), p. 43.
2. Raphael Patai, *The Hebrew Goddess* (New York: Avon, 1984), p. 222.
3. Barbara Black Koltuv, *The Book of Lilith* (York Beach, ME: Nicolas-Hays, 1986) contains many stories of Lilith's origins and deeds and a discussion of her meaning in feminine psychology.
4. Theodore H. Gaston, *The Holy and Profane* (New York: William Morrow, 1980), p. 22.
5. Patai, *The Hebrew Goddess*, p. 217.
6. Patai, *The Hebrew Goddess*, p. 213.
7. Marie-Louise von Franz, *Problems of the Feminine in Fairy Tales* (New York: Spring Publications, 1972), p. 38.
8. Marie-Louise von Franz, *Shadow and Evil in Fairy Tales* (New York: Spring Publications, 1974), p. 39.
9. Compare to the recipe in the beginning of this chapter (page 101) that begins, "Secure an egg . . ."
10. Rivkah Kluger, "The Queen of Sheba in Bible and Legend," in *Psyche and Bible* (Zurich: Spring, 1974), p. 113.
11. von Franz, *Problems of the Feminine in Fairy Tales*, p. 155.

About the Author

Dr. Barbara Black Koltuv received her Ph.D. in clinical psychology from Columbia University in 1962. She holds a diploma in psychoanalysis from the post-doctoral program at New York University, as well as a diploma and certificate as a Jungian analyst from the C.G. Jung Institute of New York. Dr. Koltuv has been a practicing analyst for more than 25 years. She specializes in matters of love, sexuality, and relationships—on both the human and archetypal realm. She currently has a private practice in New York City. She is on the Board of Directors and a faculty member of the C.G. Jung Institute, where she is a training analyst and supervisor. She has traveled extensively in Mexico, Central and South America, Europe and North Africa and has spent a great deal of time in Jerusalem. She is the mother of a daughter and a son. Dr. Koltuv is the author of the much acclaimed *Book of Lilith*, also published by Nicolas-Hays. She resides in New York City and Woodstock, New York, and is currently at work on a new book.